SS UNITED STATES

SS *United States* in Southampton Water, 4 July 1967.

SS UNITED STATES

ANDREW BRITTON

The
History
Press

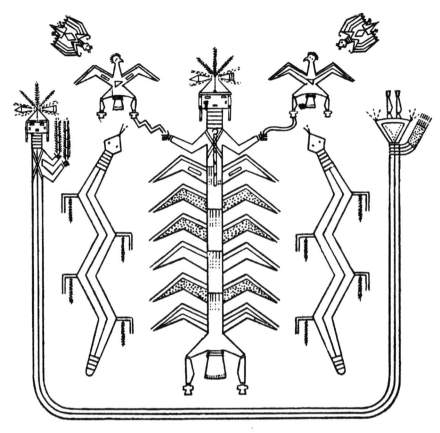

Mural from SS *United States*.

First published 2012
Reprinted 2022, 2025

The History Press
97 St George's Place,
Cheltenham, Gloucestershire, GL50 3QB
www.thehistorypress.co.uk

ISBN 978 0 7524 7953 8

Typesetting and origination by The History Press
Printed in Italy by Elcograf Spa

CONTENTS

INTRODUCTION

My first childhood memory of seeing the SS *United States* in the 1950s was of watching her emerge from the early morning mist in the Solent and pass by the Red Funnel paddle steamer I was on sailing down Southampton Water on to the Isle of Wight. I had heard much about her from my family who worked on the rival Cunard Queens, but to see her at close quarters for the first time was a treasured, unforgettable experience. The next day my father visited Southampton Docks to see my Uncle Joe on the Cunard RMS *Queen Elizabeth* and a neighbour, Sid Deeming from my home in Leamington Spa, who was working on a P&O Line cruise ship. Next door to the P&O liner at 107 Berth was the SS *United States*. After boarding the British liners, I only had one thing in mind and that was to explore the SS *United States*.

'Would you like to come aboard and have a look around?' asked a smiling SS *United States* crewman in his warm American voice.

'Yes please,' I replied. Once on board I was presented with a soft ice cream in a round cone smothered in strawberry sauce. This was a new and exciting experience for a child from England, for we had nothing like it at the time. Just minutes earlier I had sampled a solid block Walls ice cream on the Cunard RMS *Queen Elizabeth*, but it was nothing to beat this. My father explained to the crewman that he came from a Cunard family and his father was leader of the orchestra on a Cunard liner. On hearing this, it was as if we were accepted as instant members of the family. We were given a behind-the-scenes tour of the SS *United States*, including a visit to the bridge.

In 1969 I watched with my family in disbelief from Hythe Pier as the SS *United States* sailed away from Southampton into unexpected retirement.

Rumours circulated around family and friends working on the British liners that this could be the end for the SS *United States*. The question on everyone's lips was, 'Why?' She was the fastest, she was the best.

'She beat our Cunard Queens, surely the yanks won't let her go?' my Uncle Joe asked.

Years later I managed to acquire an original logbook from the SS *United States*. After making further enquiries, I discovered that most of the SS *United States* logbooks and telegraph books were available for sale. I decided to purchase as many as I could afford and preserve them. Next I set about seeking out original colour slides and the result is this book, which is about the life of the SS *United States* and commemorates the sixtieth anniversary of her construction and winning of the coveted Blue Riband for the fastest transatlantic crossing. It covers the record-breaking liner's active service from 1952 to 1969 when she dominated the seas of the Atlantic, sweeping all rivals before her. The astonishing operational capacity of this national icon of the United States, with her huge red funnels, her sleek streamlined hull and silver-coated fittings, was shrouded in secrecy in case she was ever required to be converted to a troop carrier.

Now many decades on in the twenty-first century, I try to describe to my own sons, Jonathan, Mark and Matthew, what the world's fastest liner was like; how it felt to see, hear, smell and touch the SS *United States*. I'm guilty of spending odd minutes just smelling the original engine room odour on the telegraph books and engine room logbooks I have at home. Closing my eyes, my mind drifts back through the decades and I feel I am on board the fastest ocean liner ever built.

The maiden voyage of the SS *United States*, 1952.

ACKNOWLEDGEMENTS

A huge project like this could not have come about without the help of my brother-in-law Mike Pringle, who meticulously scanned each and every slide (several thousand of them) for this series. This amounts to months of unseen hard work. Without his help, this book would not have come into being. I also owe my sister Ruth a massive thank you for all her patience and encouragement. Special thanks must go to my son Matthew for some work on the cover designs and my wife Annette for putting up with masses of colour slides, boxes of ocean liner logbooks and shipping artefacts.

Many friends have helped by allowing me to include their original work and several have generously donated their material. I am indebted to Mrs Hilda Short and the Estate of the late Pursey Short for the donation of Pursey's colour slide material of Southampton Docks. Pursey's aerial photography of the docks is second to none. Thanks also to the Estate of the late Gwyilym R. Davies for their support in acquiring the entire collection of maritime slides of this distinguished photographer. I am very grateful to Randy Holmes and the Church of Latter Day Saints, USA, for allowing me to purchase the entire Arthur Oakman original slide collection for inclusion in this and future books. Additionally the G.R. Keat and Norman Roberts slide collections have been sold to me for specific inclusion in this and future books, for which I am extremely grateful. Petroleum giants Esso and the Cunard Line have very generously given me their original slides of Southampton Docks and the liners. Some of this material will be included in future publications in this series. Similarly, I am sincerely grateful to Graham Cocks for the generous gift of all his slides to this project. Thanks must also go to the Historisches Museum Bremerhaven, R.J. 'Dick' Blenkinsop, Bryan Hicks, John Goss, David Peters, John Cox, Alan A. Jarvis, Tom Hedges, A.E. Bennett/Richard Clammer Collection, Marc Piche, Bill Di Benedetto, Pierrick Roullet of the World Ship Society, Paris Branch in France, Jim McFaul of the World Ship Society, Steamboat Bill/Steamship Historical Society of America, Harvey Sharman, Barry Eagles and John Wiltshire, who have given me permission for their fabulous original work to be included. I am very grateful to them. A special mention must be made of David Boone from the USA, alias the 'Tugboatpainter': so many of the colour slides included in the Britton Collection have originated from him. This collection also includes the outstanding slides taken by Ernest Arroyo. A very special thank you must be extended to Art Harman, who flew over to England from the USA to deliver a logbook, artefacts and slide scans for inclusion in this book. Finally, I wish to record my sincere thanks to Michael Jakeman, who cast his expert eyes over this book at the proofreading stage.

I dedicate this book to Ruby Louise Britton, the world's newest SS *United States* fan.

ABOUT THE AUTHOR

Andrew Britton first encountered the record breaking SS *United States* as a child at Southampton Docks in the 1950s. His family, who worked on the rival British Cunard Queens *Elizabeth* and *Mary*, had tipped him off about how the Big U had 'temporarily' taken the Blue Riband for the record crossing of the Atlantic. The fierce but friendly rivalry continues into the twenty-first century when he visits his family in Southampton, as they still maintain their beloved Queens could have won back this coveted trophy.

Today, Andrew is a keen supporter of the SS United States Conservancy, which has successfully preserved the liner for future generations. He is eager to see that ongoing financial contributions are flowing into the much-needed appeal funds of this irreplaceable international icon of the seas.

Andrew is a retired school teacher and a lifelong shipping enthusiast with family connections going back to the White Star Line. His grandfather, Alfred Britton, was bandmaster for the White Star Line and was due to sail aboard the ill-fated *Titanic* from Southampton, but was prevented from doing so by his grandmother who had an eerie premonition of disaster. His uncle, Norman Britton, was a popular Cunard White Star pianist and performed on many of the shipping line's ocean liners. Another uncle, Henry 'Joe' Webb, was an engineer on board the Cunard RMS *Queen Elizabeth* and he later worked in the docks. Uncle Joe's brother, Bernard Webb, worked aboard the RMS *Queen Mary* and so it could be said that Southampton shipping was in the blood.

Andrew is also passionate about steam railways and has written six books on the railways of the Isle of Wight. He has contributed to various railway enthusiast magazines and he is also the co-writer of the BBC TV documentary 'For the Love of Steam'. He is a part-owner, together with family and friends, of eight British steam locomotives that operate on the Swanage Railway and other heritage railways.

At the end of the Second World War there was an identified need for a dual-role ocean liner and US naval auxiliary ship, which could be quickly converted into a troopship within 48 hours and capable of carrying 14,000 troops over 10,000 nautical miles without refuelling. The ship was to be built for the United States Lines and constructed to rigid US Navy standards at a cost of $78 million and was partially funded for $50 million by the US Government. She was to become the largest ocean liner built in the USA and was designed to capture the Blue Riband transatlantic speed record. Her name: SS *United States*.

Work began on the construction of the SS *United States* at Newport News Shipbuilding Dry Dock Company, with the liner's keel being laid on 8 February 1950. The designer, William Francis Gibbs, was very protective about his revolutionary design information and feared it would leak out to rival shipbuilders. He determined that the only way to protect the unique hull and propeller design from curious eyes and cameras was to build the ship directly on the floor of a graving dock. This had the advantage of allowing the dry dock to be flooded, thus protecting the ship's design secrets below the waterline when it was launched; it also enabled the construction to proceed at enormous speed. Construction and assembly was therefore no longer constrained by traditional shipbuilding methods on an inclined plane with a slipway.

Modern and efficient approaches to shipbuilding and assembly learned from mass production techniques developed during the Second World War were applied to the construction of this new liner. When the SS *United States* floated off the dock floor and was towed to the final fitting-out berth for passenger accommodation to be completed, she was 70 per cent complete with nearly all of her mechanical equipment in place. All internal furnishings and fittings were custom-designed from glass, aluminium and other non-flammable, lightweight materials and built to comply to the rigid US Navy health and safety requirements. It was a well-known fact that the only wood aboard appeared in the ship's pianos and butcher blocks.

The design plan for the SS *United States* set out that the ship was to be highly compartmentalised to provide maximum flotation should there ever be a major collision or should she ever sustain damage from attack. State of the art dual-engine rooms provided the most comprehensive power output ever built into a premier passenger liner, resulting in a top speed that would remain classified for decades until she was withdrawn from service. This modern liner was built with an all-aluminium superstructure. This resulted in the SS *United States* dead weight being significantly reduced and provided the vessel a tremendous horsepower-to-weight ratio compared to her Cunard Line rivals. The sea trial logbook reveals that the SS *United States* could travel in reverse at over 21 knots, with a forward top speed of 43 knots!

On 3 July 1952, the SS *United States* sped away from United States Lines' Pier 86 in New York City and headed out into the north Atlantic to fulfil her destiny on her maiden eastbound Voyage 1. Her Master, Captain Harry Manning, Commodore of the United States Lines, encountered fog during the first day of the voyage and he cautiously reduced speed. As soon as the fog lifted, Captain Manning ordered full power and the liner responded well. The liner performed to all expectations in heavy swells and for a time exceeded 36 knots. Crossing the finishing line at Bishop's Rock, England, the SS *United States* had easily achieved the record held for fourteen years by the British Cunard RMS *Queen Mary*, arriving in an unprecedented three days, ten hours and forty minutes. On the return westbound maiden

United States at Spithead, 17 August 1967.

Voyage 1, Captain Manning pointed the liner's streamlined bow back toward the United States and once again broke all former records, arriving in New York in three days, twelve hours, twelve minutes, with an average speed for the westbound crossing of 34.51 knots.

The introduction of the transatlantic US Boeing 707 and British Comet jet aircraft in the 1950s had an enormous effect on passenger traffic for all the major ocean liners. Transatlantic travellers could fly to and from Europe in just a matter of hours instead of five or six days at sea. In the United States, subsidies began to decline, and combined with the disruption of increasingly frequent industrial disputes and strikes, on both sides of the Atlantic, the fate of ocean passenger liners appeared to be sealed. By the late 1960s, many passenger lines with dwindling passenger operations were disposing of their prestige ocean liners and Cunard pensioned off their famous *Queen Mary*, *Queen Elizabeth* and *Mauretania*.

In November 1969, the axe fell on the iconic SS *United States* when it was abruptly announced she would be withdrawn from passenger service and laid up, after an unblemished and successful seventeen-year career. There was utter shock at this devastating news on both sides of the Atlantic. Seamen in Southampton were genuinely saddened for their rivals on the 'Big U' in New York.

The SS *United States* was laid up indefinitely at Norfolk, Virginia, and she was to be sealed by the United States Navy to ensure a minimum of deterioration while laid up in the national Reserve Fleet. By 1978, the US military had decided that it had no further use for the huge liner. MARAD

offered the vessel for sale, with the stipulation made that the ship could not be sold to foreign interests, owing to the fact that the liner contained previously classified engineering features, developed in conjunction with the US military. The SS *United States* was purchased by developer Richard Hadley of Seattle. His intention was to restore her to active cruise service. When financing collapsed, the great liner's interiors and fittings were auctioned off by Guernsey's in October 1984 to pay off outstanding creditors.

The once proud SS *United States* was next purchased by a consortium owned by Fred Mayer. Several companies in the USA expressed an interest

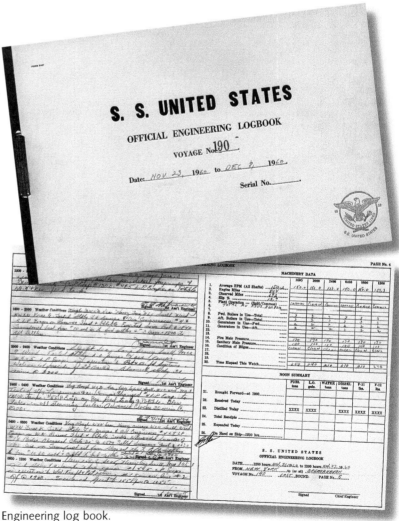

Engineering log book.

Maiden voyage, abstract log, and pre-voyage trials.

in acquiring the liner and returning it to active sea service in the Caribbean. The SS *United States* was ignominiously towed by Smits Towing Co. of Rotterdam to Turkey to enable removal of significant quantities of asbestos in June 1992. Shipyard authorities eventually seized the ship for non-payment of bills relating to the removal of hazardous materials. The Philadelphia businessman Edward Cantor stepped in and brokered a deal to resolve the ship's outstanding debt and arranged for her to be returned to the USA; she arrived in Philadelphia in July 1996. Sadly in 2003 Edward Cantor died, leaving the future of this once-iconic vessel in great doubt.

In the spring of 2003, Norwegian Cruise Line (NCL) purchased the SS *United States* as part of a multi-ship plan to create an American-flagged cruise service. Extensive feasibility studies were made which found the SS *United States* to be in remarkable structural condition despite her deteriorated outward appearance. However, in January 2009 NCL announced that it would no longer pursue a refit of the SS *United States* and that it was offering the great liner for sale. Worse news was to follow when in early 2010 NCL announced that it would be accepting bids from scrappers. Upon hearing this announcement the SS United States Conservancy launched an urgent major campaign, 'Save Our Ship', to raise funds and awareness in support of the vessel.

In July of 2010, the Conservancy announced that it had received a $5.8 million pledge from Philadelphia philanthropist H.F. 'Gerry' Lenfest. This magnificent gesture allowed the Conservancy to purchase the liner outright and maintain her at her current berth for twenty months while redevelopment plans were made and funds for her restoration were raised. For the first time in the history of the SS *United States*, a group concerned primarily with the vessel's historical significance and preservation has owned her and they now require all the funding they can muster to ensure she is preserved for future generations.

SS UNITED STATES

2

LOG RECORDS

The SS *United States* sailed exactly 400 voyages, which means exactly 800 crossings (eastbound and westbound), between June 1952 and November 1969. Here for the first time is a complete record from the original logbooks and telegraph books of the voyages of the SS *United States*.

TRIAL No.1

BUILDER'S TRIAL FROM NEWPORT NEWS, 14 MAY TO 16 MAY 1952

During the nights of 5–7 May, 53,750 barrels of Bunker C fuel were pumped aboard.

The Builder's Trials were directed under the supervision of builders. Present on the ship were bridge officers from United States Line, including Commodore Harry Manning, Captain E.D. Edwards of the Virginia Pilots Association and members of the United States House of Representatives. The total on board is recorded as 1,699 persons of which 1,200 were designated as crew.

The SS *United States* headed down the James River, passing Fort Monroe at Old Comfort Point at 09:45. A variety of equipment is recorded as being checked including navigation radio direction finder, magnetic compass, anchor windlass and rudder. During this first trial the vessel is

Loading the SS *United States*.

recorded as reaching 30 knots in oncoming 35mph winds in a choppy sea.

On Friday 16 May the trials included in the logbook are listed as: stopping, turning and manoeuvring tests.

On 7 June, the logbook records that the SS *United States* was open for public inspection.

TRIAL No.2

OFFICIAL TRIAL FROM NEWPORT NEWS 9 JUNE TO 11 JUNE 1952

The ship sailed at 06:38 with 1,704 invited guests, designated journalists and members of the Marine Administration Trial & Guarantee Safety Board to trials off the Virginia Cape. On the night of 9 June, the SS United States is recorded as having attained 39.38 knots in speed at 173rpm between 20:00 hours and 24:00 hours. The Crash Astern Test was passed at 06:50 and Crash Ahead Test passed at 07:30. The Full Speed Astern Test is recorded as 22.7 knots.

On 10 September between 08:00 hours and 12:00 hours the SS United States achieved 43 knots at 188rpm using the two booster and two main feed pumps in the forward and after engine rooms.

12 June: Vessel in dry dock for inspection to the propellers having collided with floating debris during the trial. No damage discovered.

20 JUNE TO 23 JUNE 1952 NEWPORT NEWS TO NEW YORK

09:42 Commodore Harry Manning of the United States Line formally signed to accept the vessel on behalf of United States Line at Newport News Shipyard. Thereafter, fire drill procedure was conducted and fuel pumping on to the ship.

Depart Newport News Shipyard at 05:44 on 22 June.
During the short voyage from Newport News into Pier 86 at New York, the SS United States attained a speed of 33 knots with 1,200 invited guests on board. The liner was escorted from the Narrows at 07:05 by the US Navy destroyers USS Warrington, Perry, Goodrich and W.M. Wood – two in front and two astern formation. A cavalcade of unofficial vessels escorted the SS United States into port with noisy salutes.

The vessel was opened to public inspection from 10:00 on Saturday 28 June at a cost of $1 per adult and 50 cents per child.

The Cunard RMS Queen Elizabeth arrived at New York Pier 90 on 30 June and Captain G. Cove lowered the ship's ensign as a salute. This was reciprocated by the SS United States. Captain Cove later visited the SS United States to present a pennant and goodwill message to Commodore Manning.

The Engineering logbook records that Esso pumped in 9,650 tons of bunker C fuel oil in readiness for the maiden voyage on 2 July 1952.

VOYAGE 1 Maiden Voyage Eastbound 3 July to 9 July 1952 New York to Le Havre to Southampton (Award of Blue Riband for eastbound crossing).

Westbound 11 July to 14 July 1952, Southampton to Le Havre to New York (Award of Blue Riband for westbound crossing).

On the first day of the maiden voyage the SS United States averaged a speed of 34.11 knots and travelled 696 nautical miles. The next day she bettered this with an average speed of 35.6 knots covering 801 nautical miles. The third day was hampered by fog and poor visibility, but the liner covered a remarkable distance of 814 nautical miles. During the eastbound maiden voyage on Sunday 5 July, the SS United States passed the French Line Liberté, which had formerly held the transatlantic Blue Riband record when originally named Europa. The SS United States also passed her running mate the SS America crossing in the opposite direction to New York. There was an impressive whistle salute from both ships as crowds lined the decks to witness the occasion.

Extreme caution was maintained in the fog and the SS United States relied upon her twin sets of radar. As the fog lifted on Monday 6 July, a stiff wind developed resulting in a choppy sea. At 17:00 the SS United States passed the Cunard RMS Queen Mary at a distance of 11 miles. The telegram received on the bridge by Commodore Manning from Captain Harry Grattidge on the Queen Mary read, 'Welcome to the family of big liners on the Atlantic.'

Speed on the third day increased to an average of 36.17 knots covering 814 nautical miles. The engineering logbook states that all propeller shafts were turning at an incredible 165.5rpm! The SS United States was recorded in the logbook as passing Bishop's Rock at 05:16 (Greenwich Mean Time) on Monday 7 July. The voyage took 3 days, 10 hours, 40 minutes, averaging 35.59 knots. This was an incredible record-breaking achievement, bettering the Queen Mary's previous best by 10 hours, 2 minutes, over the 2,949 nautical miles. Commodore Manning ordered the ship's whistle to be sounded with three long blasts. The band of the SS United States played, 'The Star Spangled Banner', whilst passengers and crew cheered and danced a conga around the decks.

The SS United States arrived ahead of schedule at Le Havre and was advised to anchor for 5 hours outside to await pier allocation the next morning at 12:24. The logbook records that local French Harbour Pilots Messieurs Albert Guerrier and George Dubois joined the ship to see her safely into port for the maiden docking. It was observed by the distinguished French maritime enthusiast Monsieur Pierrick Roullet that upon arrival in Le Havre, the SS United States' new paintwork had flaked on the forward shell plating owing to the high speeds on the voyage. The logbook also records that there was 2ft 6in less of draft at the aft owing to the fuel consumed!

Departing from Le Havre at 12:46, the SS United States passed the British Royal Navy aircraft carrier HMS Indomitable. The band of the Royal Marines on the flight deck wryly played a salute of, 'Rule Britannia, Britannia rules the waves' followed by loaded cheers from the raucous British sailors. A US Navy destroyer escorted the SS United States across the English Channel. At the Nab Tower, off Ryde on the Isle of Wight, the SS United States took on local Trinity House Pilot James Bowyer. Heading down Southampton Water, the watching crowds at Hythe Pier were treated to the sound of a bagpiper perched on the forecastle of the SS United States. At the point of entering the Ocean Dock, passenger James Black broke into a rendition of 'The Black Bear'. The arrival in Southampton was amazing, according to Southampton ocean liner enthusiast John Britton, who was present. 'She was escorted by a huge flotilla of Red Funnel paddle steamers, tugs and pleasure craft with crowds lining the shores and docks to catch a first glimpse.' Once safely docked at the Ocean Terminal, the SS United States was welcomed by the Mayor of Southampton, Alderman Edwin Burrow. The Borough of Southampton Police Band serenaded the passengers of the new Blue Riband winner from the dockside.

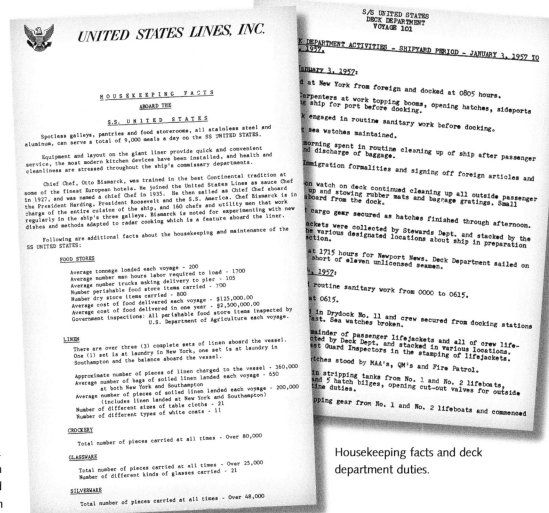

Housekeeping facts and deck department duties.

The departure from Southampton was at 16:00 on 10 July, returning to Le Havre with 1,617 passengers. After departing Le Havre at 01:00, the SS United States passed Bishop's Rock at 09:17 on her eastbound maiden voyage. The logbook records speed rapidly increasing to 36.08 knots with all propeller shafts responding from 160rpm to an average of 177.4rpm. On the second day of the westbound maiden voyage fog was encountered and speed slightly reduced to an average of 33.95 knots over the 865 nautical miles covered. With a smooth sea and hazy vision, the performance of the ship increased the next day

with an average speed of 34.19 knots over 872 nautical miles. The record-breaking voyage concluded at Ambrose Light Ship at 16:29 on 14 July. The SS United States had won the Blue Riband for the westbound crossing of the Atlantic in 3 days, 12 hours, 12 minutes, covering the 2,906 miles from Bishop's Rock to Ambrose Light Ship.

After being held at anchor overnight off the Quarantine Station at Staten Island for Federal inspection, the SS United States triumphantly headed into New York towards Pier 86 at 07:10. Flying a 40ft-long blue banner from the radar mast, which was presented by the press corps, the ship was escorted into port with a noisy reception from an armada of local boats all profusely whistling salutes. She finally docked at 09:12 and was welcomed by the traditional jet spray salute from the fireboats with the Fire Department Band playing at the end of Pier 86.

VOYAGE 2 Eastbound and Westbound New York to Le Havre to Southampton to Le Havre to New York, 23 July to 4 August 1952.

VOYAGE 3 Eastbound and Westbound New York to Le Havre to Southampton to Le Havre to New York, 8 August to 21 August 1952.

The passenger list booklet for Voyage 3 contained some well-known celebrities including film star and comedian Bob Hope, Lawrence Rockefeller and his family, Secretary of Commerce Charles Sawyer and several US senators.

VOYAGE 4 Eastbound and Westbound New York to Le Havre to Southampton to Le Havre to New York, 22 August to 3 September 1952.

An announcement was made on board the SS *United States* to inform passengers and crew that US Line was extending their voyages on the ship to Bremerhaven in Germany for the remainder of the schedule for the year. The westbound voyage encountered heavy storms, but the ship returned back to New York on schedule.

VOYAGE 5 Eastbound and Westbound New York to Le Havre to Southampton to Le Havre to New York, 5 September to 18 September 1952.

The passenger list booklet records that Hollywood stars Adolphe Menjou, Buster Keaton and Rita Hayworth were on board. From the political world, the Speaker of the Canadian House of Commons and Senator Beauregard were also present, travelling first class.

VOYAGE 6 Eastbound and Westbound New York to Le Havre to Southampton to Le Havre to New York, 19 September to 1 October 1952.

VOYAGE 7 Eastbound and Westbound New York to Le Havre to Southampton to Le Havre to New York, 2 October to 16 October 1952.

VOYAGE 8 Eastbound and Westbound New York to Le Havre to Southampton to Le Havre to New York, 17 October to 29 October 1952.

Arrival in New York was delayed on this voyage by 7 hours due to a reduction in speed during a mid-Atlantic storm with 75mph winds encountered.

VOYAGE 9 Eastbound and Westbound New York to Le Havre to Southampton to Le Havre to New York, 31 October to 11 November 1952.

The passenger list records the Duke of Sutherland was aboard for this voyage and the 4ft-high solid silver Hales Trophy was delivered aboard. This magnificent trophy was awarded to the record-breaking vessel for the fastest crossing of the Atlantic. Presentation of the Hales Trophy was made by the Duke of Sutherland to Commodore Manning and General Franklin of the United States Line at 19:30 on 12 November.

VOYAGE 10 Eastbound and Westbound New York to Le Havre to Southampton to Le Havre to New York, 12 November to 26 November 1952.

Arrival at Pier 86 coincided with a longshoreman strike and passengers were advised by the Purser that they could only take off such luggage as they could remove by hand. All remaining larger items including the mail and cargo would be removed from the ship at Newport News.

To Newport News Dry Dock on Thursday 27 November 1952.

Departed from Pier 86, New York, at 14:33 on 27 November.

Arrived at Newport News Dry Dock at 18:10 on 27 November.

Inspection of the ship in dry dock revealed no significant problems with the hull and propellers. The hull was repainted and passenger carrying modifications were implemented by removing the third berth in many cabins and assigning more space for crew.

Departed from Newport News at 07:00 on 7 December.

Arrived at Pier 86, New York, at 11:31 on 7 December.

VOYAGE 11 Eastbound and Westbound New York to Le Havre to Southampton to Le Havre to New York, 9 December 1952 to 23 December 1952.

Whilst un-docking for departure to Le Havre at Southampton on 17 December, 83mph south-westerly cross winds caught the funnels causing the ship to be dragged for a distance of over 200 yards. This caused damage to the paintwork and a minor dent to the bridge wing. Seven tugs were instructed to assist from Red Funnel and Alexandra Towing Company under the direction of the Pilot. After 53 minutes, the SS *United States* was returned to berth and secured for inspection. She departed 20 hours later.

The SS *United States* arrived in New York on schedule, but according to the logbook was unusually docked at Pier 61, before being transferred to Pier 86 for preparations for Voyage 12.

VOYAGE 12 Eastbound and Westbound New York to Le Havre to Southampton to Bremerhaven to Southampton to Le Havre to New York, 27 December 1952 to 10 January 1953.

This was the maiden voyage into Bremerhaven on 3 January 1953. Mr Kenneth Gautier, vice president for passenger traffic of the United States Line and the SS *United States,* was welcomed by Burgermeister Wilhelm Kaisen die Festrede.

VOYAGE 13 Eastbound and Westbound New York to Le Havre to Southampton to Bremerhaven to Southampton to Le Havre to New York, 14 January to 28 January 1953.

The passenger list for this voyage includes His Royal Highness Prince Axel and his wife Her Royal Highness Princess Margaretha of Denmark, and Her Majesty Queen Tadj ol-Molouk, Queen Consort of late Reza Shah Pahlavi of Iran, accompanied by her daughter, Her Imperial Royal Highness Princess Ashraf.

VOYAGE 14 Eastbound and Westbound New York to Le Havre to Southampton to Bremerhaven to Southampton to Le Havre to New York, 31 January to 15 February 1953.

Gales and severe weather conditions forced a 24-hour delay in sailing from Le Havre until 11 February. Unsuccessful attempts via the shell door were made to allow the transfer of the Le Havre Harbour Pilot Monsieur George du Bois. It was therefore decided to abort this and the French Pilot to remained on board for the remainder of the voyage to New York.

VOYAGE 15 Eastbound and Westbound New York to Le Havre to Southampton to Bremerhaven to Southampton to Le Havre to New York, 18 February to 5 March 1953.

The passenger list records Lord Ismay, son of the *Titanic* disaster survivor and former chairman of the White Star Line, as being on board.

Mid-Atlantic on 2 March at 12:02, the speed of the ship was reduced to 110rpm in order to ease heavy pitching in a storm. All passengers and crew advised to remain secure during the storm. Full speed resumed at 18:07.

VOYAGE 16 Eastbound and Westbound New York to Le Havre to Southampton to Bremerhaven to Southampton to Le Havre to New York, 7 March to 21 March 1953.

VOYAGE 17 Eastbound and Westbound New York to Le Havre to Southampton to Le Havre to New York, 25 March to 6 April 1953.

VOYAGE 18 Eastbound and Westbound New York to Le Havre to Southampton to Le Havre to New York, 9 April to 21 April 1953.

The logbook contraband and narcotics search identified SS *United States* Porter George Salas Silva and United States Line employee Bernard V Schuman arrested off the ship for smuggling 33 ounces of pure fine heroin aboard.

VOYAGE 19 Eastbound and Westbound New York to Le Havre to Southampton to Le Havre to New York, 24 April to 5 May 1953.

VOYAGE 20 Eastbound and Westbound New York to Le Havre to Southampton to Le Havre to New York, 8 May to 19 May 1953.

VOYAGE 21 Eastbound and Westbound New York to Le Havre to Southampton to Le Havre to New York, 22 May to 2 June 1953.

His Royal Highness The Duke of Windsor and his wife, the former Wallis Simpson, were aboard for this voyage and allocated to Suite U87-89, popularly known as the 'Duck Suite'. The Duke and Duchess of Windsor had previously always travelled on the Cunard Queen liners. The Duchess of Windsor stated that, 'Cunard treated us like English snobs, with contempt as my husband had abdicated.' Perhaps the true reason was that the United States Line allowed the Windsors to pay only the minimum first class fare on the SS *United States* and this would be upgraded immediately at no extra cost for the special suite. 'Cunard expected us to pay the full rate,' the duchess pointed out.

The Duke of Windsor was given a unique privilege of unlimited access to the bridge of the SS *United States*. He would always take advantage of this when approaching Bishop's Rock to view the English coast. The Windsors frequently travelled on the SS *United States* after this voyage between Le Havre and New York. The routine was that they would be driven from their home in France in a limousine to Le Havre for immediate VIP boarding on to the liner. They would be accompanied by a Citroën van containing up to 100 pieces of luggage.

After boarding the SS *United States*, the Windsors settled down to a Cognac brandy and cocktail served by the duke's valet. Almost uniquely, their five pet pug dogs would remain with the Windsors throughout the day. The crew of the SS *United States* would often muse at the collars of these dogs which had gold sovereigns in them! The duke's valet and the duchess's maid would usually be provided with an allocation of three nearby inside cabins.

The Windsors could often be seen on board dancing, playing bingo in the main lounge and dining. According to the crew, the duke would lament about ocean liners and ships of the Royal Navy, whereas the duchess would discuss social niceties. Once when the queen of cosmetics, Estée Lauder, was on board she requested to meet her. The Windsors never again travelled across the Atlantic by any other liner than the SS *United States*.

VOYAGE 22 Eastbound and Westbound New York to Le Havre to Southampton to Le Havre to New York, 5 June to 16 June 1953.

VOYAGE 23 Eastbound and Westbound New York to Le Havre to Southampton to Le Havre to New York, 26 June to 7 July 1953.

VOYAGE 24 Eastbound and Westbound New York to Le Havre to Southampton to Le Havre to New York, 10 July to 21 July 1953.

VOYAGE 25 Eastbound and Westbound New York to Le Havre to Southampton to Le Havre to New York, 24 July to 4 August 1953.

VOYAGE 26 Eastbound and Westbound New York to Le Havre to Southampton to Le Havre to New York, 7 August to 18 August 1953.

VOYAGE 27 Eastbound and Westbound New York to Le Havre to Southampton to Le Havre to New York, 21 August to 1 September 1953.

VOYAGE 28 Eastbound and Westbound New York to Le Havre to Southampton to Le Havre to New York, 4 September to 15 September 1953.

VOYAGE 29 Eastbound and Westbound New York to Le Havre to Southampton to Le Havre to New York, 17 September to 28 September 1953.

Their Royal Majesties King Paul and Queen Frederika of Greece are listed on the passenger list booklet and are recorded as having accepted an invitation from the captain to join him for cocktails and a dinner.

VOYAGE 30 Eastbound and Westbound New York to Le Havre to Southampton to Le Havre to New York, 30 September to 11 October 1953.

VOYAGE 31 Eastbound and Westbound New York to Le Havre to Southampton to Le Havre to New York, 16 October to 28 October 1953.

VOYAGE 32 Eastbound and Westbound New York to Le Havre to Southampton to Le Havre to New York, 31 October to 12 November 1953.

VOYAGE 33 Eastbound and Westbound New York to Le Havre to Southampton to Bremerhaven to Southampton to Le Havre to New York, 17 November to 1 December 1953.

VOYAGE 34 Eastbound and Westbound New York to Le Havre and Plymouth to Bremerhaven to Southampton to Le Havre to New York, 4 December to 18 December 1953.

Wednesday 9 December 1953 The tug men at Southampton Docks went on strike for the second time in 1953 and therefore the SS *United States* diverted to Plymouth on the evening of Wednesday 9 December 1953 to land her passengers. Two trains were arranged to take them from Millbay Docks at 8 p.m. and 9 p.m. to London Waterloo, where they were due at 1.41 a.m. and 2.41 a.m. respectively. However, disembarkation was delayed and the Statesman special train did not arrive at Waterloo until 5.15 a.m. the following morning.

15 December The logbook reports 00:00 to 04:00 a very rough southeasterly sea and heavy confused SXE and southwesterly swell. This resulted in the SS *United States* taking water over the decks and hatches. The vessel is reported in the logbook as rolling 24 degrees to port and 26 degrees to starboard. By 15:32 the storm worsened to storm force 11 with the vessel deeply pitching in mountainous seas. Consequently, speed was reduced to just 11 knots with just 70rpm on the propeller. At 24:00 the logbook records the ship in very rough northerly sea as rolling to a maximum of 30 degrees to port and 15 to starboard. This resulted in an 11-hour-delayed arrival into New York.

The ship departed from New York at 13:52 hours on 19 December to Hampton Roads, Portsmouth Naval Dockyard, arrival 03:51 hours to anchor off dead, and awaiting tugs.

The ship entered Dry Dock 21 December at 08:41 hours. The vessel was in position at 09:31 hours and on the blocks fore and aft at 11:50 hours, dock dry at 15:20 hours. Full inspection of the hull commenced. Damage was reported to blade edges of Nos 3 and 4 propellers.

The rudder was tested and repairs effected. The work undertaken in addition to the routine repaint comprised replacement of boiler tubes, tube plate, stays, replacement of propellers and bow reinforcement with epoxy resin and internal refurbishment.

Full repaint and intermediate overhaul commenced at 15:20 hours until 16:00 hours on 7 January 1954. The vessel departed from Portsmouth at 13:32 on 8 January 1954, arrival at New York 04:53 on 9 January 1954.

VOYAGE 35 Eastbound and Westbound New York to Le Havre to Southampton to Bremerhaven to Southampton to Le Havre to New York, 15 January to 29 January 1954.

VOYAGE 36 Eastbound and Westbound New York to Le Havre to Southampton to Bremerhaven to Southampton to Le Havre to New York, 2 February to 16 February 1954.

VOYAGE 37 Eastbound and Westbound New York to Le Havre to Southampton to Bremerhaven to Southampton to Le Havre to New York, 16 February to 4 March 1954.

Christian evangelist Billy Graham was on the passenger list bound for the Great London Crusade of 1 March 1954. Billy sailed for England and was invited by the captain to preach to passengers and crew. The ballroom of the SS United States was packed to capacity and overflowing. The next morning aboard ship on 22 February 1954, the captain handed a devastating telegram to Billy Graham:

A Labour Member of Parliament announced today that he would challenge in Commons the admission of Billy Graham to England on the grounds the American evangelist was interfering in British politics under the guise of religion.

This was referring to the fact that a Crusade brochure had mentioned the woes brought on by socialism. The British Labour Party took it as an attack. Momentarily, Billy Graham felt the crusade was ruined. Yet God had led him this far: he would go on. Billy prayed quietly in his cabin alone on the SS United States and then sent an apology. When he disembarked from the SS United States at Southampton he was mobbed by hostile tabloid reporters. He said he believed God was going to pour out revival upon England. As he passed through customs, a US Lines agent and a Southampton dock worker thanked him for coming, as did a local taxi driver. Billy's spirits lifted.

VOYAGE 38 Eastbound and Westbound New York to Le Havre to Southampton to Bremerhaven to Southampton to Le Havre to New York, 6 March to 20 March 1954.

6 March At 09:32 lifeboat No.24 was dropped from the sun deck to the water during a routine fire drill at Pier 86, New York. Extensive damage to the lifeboat is recorded in the logbook and the six crew members were injured, requiring first-aid treatment for critical injuries to the head and neck, as well as attention for nose bleeding, cracked ribs, arms, ankle, cuts and bruises. All six members of crew were taken to St Claire's Hospital, West 51st Street, where one member of crew died. The logbook states that the accident was due to the negligent act of a crew member in prematurely operating the release lever.

11 March Upon arrival at Le Havre, the SS United States had achieved a very fast crossing of 3 days, 20 hours and 57minutes. The highlight of the eastbound voyage was on 9 March when the vessel averaged 32.36 knots covering 728 nautical miles. This figure included a sustained burst of speed at 34 knots.

20 March Owing to a longshoremen's industrial dispute, volunteer staff assisted SS United States with docking and unloading baggage at New York.

VOYAGE 39 Eastbound and Westbound New York to Le Havre to Southampton to Bremerhaven to Southampton to Le Havre to New York, 24 March to 7 April 1954.

26 March The logbook records the sudden death of Chief Purser John Lock, aged fifty-eight years. As his body was too big for any of the ship's coffins, it was stored packed in ice within a bath in the ship's hospital until arrival at New York.

VOYAGE 40 Eastbound and Westbound New York to Le Havre to Southampton to Bremerhaven to Southampton to Le Havre to New York, 10 April to 26 April 1954.

VOYAGE 41 Eastbound and Westbound New York to Le Havre to Southampton to Le Havre to New York, 30 April to 11 May 1954.

VOYAGE 42 Eastbound and Westbound New York to Le Havre to Southampton to Le Havre to New York, 14 May to 25 May 1954.

Haile Selassie, Emperor of Ethiopia, was on board and gave a rail-side interview on the ship to a CBS television reporter. The filming of this scoop was conducted from an approaching tugboat!

VOYAGE 43 Eastbound and Westbound New York to Le Havre to Southampton to Le Havre to New York, 28 May to 8 June 1954.

VOYAGE 44 Eastbound and Westbound New York to Le Havre to Southampton to Le Havre to New York, 11 June to 22 June 1954.

VOYAGE 45 Eastbound and Westbound New York to Le Havre to Southampton to Le Havre to New York, 25 June to 6 July 1954.

VOYAGE 46 Eastbound and Westbound New York to Le Havre to Southampton to Le Havre to New York, 7 July to 19 July 1954.

Transfer to Bayonne Naval Dockyard Dry Dock No.4 for attention to the propellers and sand blasting/repaint of hull, 19 July to 22 July 1954. The ship was shaft tested and passed fit for purpose and the hull cleaned and repainted. Thereafter, she returned to Pier 86 at New York at 09:40 on 22 July 1954.

VOYAGE 47 Eastbound and Westbound New York to Le Havre to Southampton to Le Havre to New York, 24 July to 4 August 1954.

VOYAGE 48 Eastbound and Westbound New York to Le Havre to Southampton to Le Havre to New York, 6 August to 17 August 1954.

VOYAGE 49 Eastbound and Westbound New York to Le Havre to Southampton to Le Havre to New York, 20 August to 31 August 1954.

The ship docked at Pier 86 during Hurricane Carol, Force 9–10 wind strength causing damage sustained to hull plating. Five Moran tugs were brought in to assist with docking instead of the usual three tugs, under the direction of Captain Frederick W. Snyder, senior Moran docking pilot.

VOYAGE 50 Eastbound and Westbound New York to Cherbourg to Southampton to Cherbourg to New York. 3 September to 14 September 1954.

A stowaway was discovered on board soon after sailing from New York on 3 September. He was identified as eleven-year-old Eugene Hart of 18 Schaeffer Street, Brooklyn. He explained that he had been given 17 cents by his grandmother, warned not to go too far and return in good

time for lunch. Spotting that the SS *United States* was due to sail at midday in the newspaper, he rushed over to look around her. 'I was still looking around her when I found the ship was at sea. I didn't know who to tell or whether I should tell all,' he explained. He was discovered at boat drill without a life jacket and placed in the ship's hospital under 24-hour guard until his return to New York.

The unusual detour to Cherbourg recorded in the logbook was due to an industrial dispute at Le Havre.

VOYAGE 51 Eastbound and Westbound New York to Le Havre to Southampton to Le Havre to New York, 17 September to 28 September 1954.

VOYAGE 52 Eastbound and Westbound New York to Le Havre to Southampton to Le Havre to New York, 30 September to 11 October 1954.

VOYAGE 53 Eastbound and Westbound New York to Le Havre to New York, 15 October to 26 October 1954.

The ship arrived at Le Havre at 06:48 on 20 October, transfer movement at 07:54, departed 02:02 on 22 October and did not call at Southampton, owing to strike action. Arrival at New York was delayed by 11 hours owing to 73mph headwinds in a gale.

VOYAGE 54 Eastbound and Westbound New York to Le Havre to Southampton to Le Havre to New York, 29 October to 9 November 1954.

The passenger list recorded the Duke and Duchess of Windsor, aboard again with five dogs and seventy-eight items of luggage.

VOYAGE 55 Eastbound and Westbound New York to Le Havre to Southampton to Bremerhaven to Southampton to Le Havre to New York, 12 November to 26 November 1954.

Hollywood superstar Marlon Brando and artist Salvador Dali were on the VIP list of passengers on this voyage.

VOYAGE 56 Eastbound and Westbound New York to Le Havre to Southampton to Bremerhaven to Le Havre to New York, 1 December to 15 December 1954.

The vessel was held at anchor at Bremerhaven from 21:45 on 7 December to 14:13 on 9 December with main engine lubricator problem. After arrival at New York, the ship was transferred at 17:53 on 15 December to Hampton

Press releases.

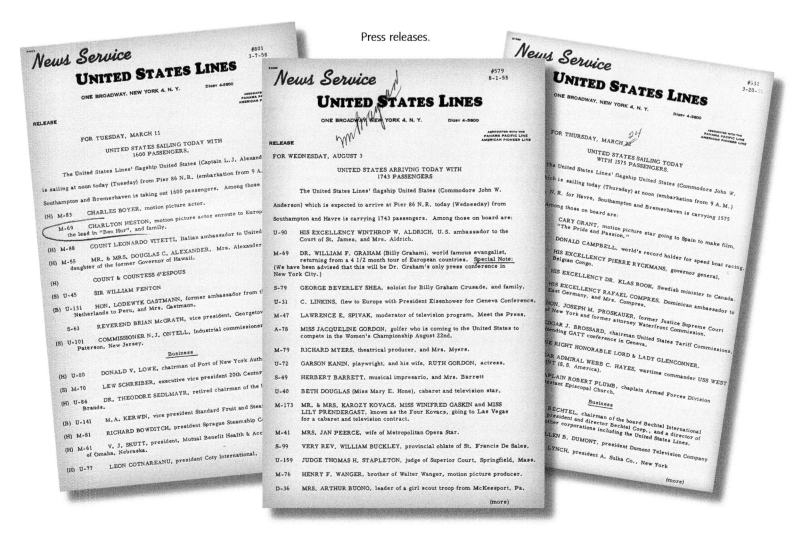

Roads, arriving at 07:41 to the dry dock at Newport News, released and transferred to New York on 7 January 1955. Work in the dry dock included the application to the bow and stern of a coating of formula Z16 neoprene, which was designed to reduce friction and prevent saltwater corrosion.

VOYAGE 57 Eastbound and Westbound New York to Le Havre to Southampton to Bremerhaven to Le Havre to New York, 13 January to 28 January 1955.

22 January at Dover Straits 13:01 to 13:35, on 22 January diverted to Le Havre, thence to Southampton before returning to New York.

Arrival at Southampton on 19 January was delayed by 24 hours owing to 82mph head winds.

VOYAGE 58 Eastbound and Westbound New York to Le Havre to Southampton to Bremerhaven to Southampton to Le Havre to New York, 1 February to 15 February 1955.

VOYAGE 59 Eastbound and Westbound New York to Le Havre to Southampton to Bremerhaven to Le Havre to New York, 18 February to 4 March 1955.

VOYAGE 60 Eastbound and Westbound New York to Le Havre to Southampton to Bremerhaven to Le Havre to New York, 8 March to 22 March 1955.

21 March United States Customs officers arrested Alexander Pruzan from Brewster, New York, in possession in his luggage of $82,000-worth of Swiss watches and 339 bottles of French perfume. Mr Pruzan declared that he was unaware of any customs restrictions and duty payable, as they were a business investment!

VOYAGE 61 Eastbound and Westbound New York to Le Havre to Southampton to Bremerhaven to Le Havre to New York, 24 March to 7 April 1955.

VOYAGE 62 Eastbound and Westbound New York to Le Havre to Southampton to Bremerhaven to Le Havre to New York, 9 April to 23 April 1955.
   The passenger list booklet includes the Duke and Duchess of Windsor.

VOYAGE 63 Eastbound and Westbound New York to Le Havre to Southampton to Le Havre to New York, 27 April to 9 May 1955.

VOYAGE 64 Eastbound and Westbound New York to Le Havre to Southampton to Le Havre to New York, 12 May to 23 May 1955.

VOYAGE 65 Eastbound and Westbound New York to Le Havre to Southampton to Le Havre to New York, 26 May to 6 June 1955.

VOYAGE 66 Eastbound and Westbound New York to Le Havre to Southampton to Le Havre to New York, 10 June to 21 June 1955.

VOYAGE 67 Eastbound and Westbound New York to Le Havre to Southampton to Le Havre to New York, 24 June to 5 July 1955.

VOYAGE 68 Eastbound and Westbound New York to Le Havre to Southampton to Le Havre to New York, 7 July to 18 July 1955.
   The vessel departed from Pier 86 to Bayonne Naval Base at 19:18 on 18 July for dry dock inspection, repaint and intermediate overhaul. The ship departed from dry dock at 10:24 on 21 July returning to Pier 86, New York, on 21 July 1955.
   The hull, propellers and rudder were checked, and tubes replaced and corked. Repainting internally and externally commenced.

VOYAGE 69 Eastbound and Westbound New York to Le Havre to Southampton to Le Havre to New York, 23 July to 3 August 1955.

VOYAGE 70 Eastbound and Westbound New York to Le Havre to Southampton to Le Havre to New York, 5 August to 16 August 1955.
   The log book states, 'Detention at sea due to emergency bells, at standby 15:30 to 16:50' on 13 August 1955. There is no recorded explanation for this unexplained action.

VOYAGE 71 Eastbound and Westbound New York to Le Havre to Southampton to Le Havre to New York, 19 August to 30 August 1955.

VOYAGE 72 Eastbound and Westbound New York to Le Havre to Southampton to Le Havre to New York, 2 September to 13 September 1955.

VOYAGE 73 Eastbound and Westbound New York to Le Havre to Southampton to Le Havre to New York, 16 September to 27 September 1955.

VOYAGE 74 Eastbound and Westbound New York to Le Havre to Southampton to Le Havre to New York, 30 September to 11 October 1955.
   The logbook states that speed was reduced on 4 October 10:00 to 11:11 whilst at sea.

VOYAGE 75 Eastbound and Westbound New York to Le Havre to Southampton to Le Havre to New York, 14 October to 25 October.

VOYAGE 76 Eastbound and Westbound New York to Le Havre to Southampton to Bremerhaven to Southampton to Le Havre to New York, 28 October to 11 November 1955.

VOYAGE 77 Eastbound and Westbound New York to Le Havre to Southampton to Bremerhaven to Southampton to Le Havre to New York, 15 November to 29 November 1955.
   The vessel sustained damage from heavy weather on 23, 27 and 28 November 1955. There were also a number of recorded complaints from passengers owing to seasickness.

VOYAGE 78 Eastbound and Westbound New York to Le Havre to Southampton to Bremerhaven to Southampton to Le Havre to New York, 2 December to 16 December 1955.

The ship departed from Pier 86, New York, at 19:39 on 16 December. The vessel arrived at Newport News at 04:44 on 17 December 1955 and departed at 18:38 on 5 January 1956. The ship returned to Pier 86, New York, at 05:33 on 6 January 1956.

In addition to routine overhaul requirements, two cinemascope screens were installed into the first- and tourist-class theatres.

VOYAGE 79 Eastbound and Westbound New York to Le Havre to Southampton to Bremerhaven to Southampton to Le Havre to New York, 11 January to 25 January 1956.

VOYAGE 80 Eastbound and Westbound New York to Le Havre to Southampton to Bremerhaven to Southampton to Le Havre to New York, 28 January to 11 February 1956.

VOYAGE 81 Eastbound and Westbound New York to Le Havre to Southampton to Bremerhaven to Southampton to Le Havre to New York, 16 February to 1 March 1956.

VOYAGE 82 Eastbound and Westbound New York to Le Havre to Southampton to Bremerhaven to Southampton to Le Havre to New York, 6 March to 20 March 1956.

VOYAGE 83 Eastbound and Westbound New York to Le Havre to Southampton to Bremerhaven to Southampton to Le Havre to New York, 22 March to 5 April 1956.

VOYAGE 84 Eastbound and Westbound New York to Le Havre to Southampton to Bremerhaven to Southampton to Le Havre to New York, 7 April to 21 April 1956.

VOYAGE 85 Eastbound and Westbound New York to Le Havre to Southampton to Le Havre to New York, 25 April to 7 May 1956.

VOYAGE 86 Eastbound and Westbound New York to Le Havre to Southampton to Le Havre to New York, 11 May to 22 May 1956.

Former President of the United States Harry S. Truman and Mrs Truman were amongst the first-class passengers on board. They used the Duck Suite rooms U87–89, which were usually used by the Duke and Duchess of Windsor.

VOYAGE 87 Eastbound and Westbound New York to Le Havre to Southampton to Le Havre to New York, 25 May to 5 June 1956.

VOYAGE 88 Eastbound and Westbound New York to Le Havre to Southampton to Le Havre to New York, 8 June to 19 June 1956.

VOYAGE 89 Eastbound and Westbound New York to Le Havre to Southampton to Le Havre to New York, 22 June to 3 July 1956.

VOYAGE 90 Eastbound and Westbound New York to Le Havre to Southampton to Le Havre to New York, 6 July to 17 July 1956.

VOYAGE 91 Eastbound and Westbound New York to Le Havre to Southampton to Le Havre to New York, 19 July to 30 July 1956.

The vessel departed from Pier 86, New York to Bayonne Naval Shipyard at 19:07 on 30 July arrived at Bayonne Naval Shipyard at 20:21 on 30 July.

The ship departed Bayonne Naval Dockyard at 05:12 on 2 August 1956 returning to Pier 86, New York at 07:35 on 2 August 1956.

VOYAGE 92 Eastbound and Westbound New York to Le Havre to Southampton to Le Havre to New York, 4 August to 15 August 1956.

VOYAGE 93 Eastbound and Westbound New York to Le Havre to Southampton to Le Havre to New York, 17 August to 28 August.

The passenger list contained His Royal Highness Prince Rainier and Princess Grace of Monaco.

VOYAGE 94 Eastbound and Westbound New York to Le Havre to Southampton to Le Havre to New York, 31 August to 11 September 1956.

VOYAGE 95 Eastbound and Westbound New York to Le Havre to Southampton to Cherbourg to New York, 14 September to 25 September 1956.

VOYAGE 96 Eastbound and Westbound New York to Le Havre to Southampton to Le Havre to New York, 28 September to 9 October 1956.

VOYAGE 97 Eastbound and Westbound New York to Le Havre to Southampton to Le Havre to New York, 11 October to 22 October 1956.

VOYAGE 98 Eastbound and Westbound New York to Le Havre to Southampton to Bremerhaven to Le Havre to New York, 26 October to 9 November 1956.

VOYAGE 99 Eastbound and Westbound New York to Le Havre to Southampton to Bremerhaven to Le Havre to New York, 13 November to 27 November 1956.

The passenger list included actress Merle Oberon and Salvador Dali.

VOYAGE 100 Eastbound and Westbound New York to Le Havre to Southampton to Bremerhaven to Le Havre to New York, 29 November to 13 December 1956.

On this 100th voyage was film star Rita Hayworth.

VOYAGE 101 Eastbound and Westbound New York to Le Havre to Southampton to Bremerhaven to Le Havre to New York, 17 December 1956 to 3 January 1957.

Depart Pier 86, New York at 17:15 on 3 January, arrive at Newport News Dry Dock No.4 at 04:40 on 4 January. Depart Newport News at 21:21 on 17 January, arrive at Pier 86, New York, at 06:28 on 18 January 1957.

VOYAGE 102 Eastbound and Westbound New York to Le Havre to Southampton to Bremerhaven to Le Havre to New York, 23 January to 7 February 1957.

Distinguished passengers on board for this voyage included Mr and Mrs Yehudi Menuhin and John L. Lewis, president of the United Mine Workers.

At 09:25 the SS *United States* was required to dock at slack water in between the tides unassisted owing to a tug strike. At 09:33 longshoremen on the pier caught the lead line thrown from the ship. This was attached to a 10in hawser. At 09:40 the hawser was made fast to a bollard ready for the SS *United States* to winch herself in. By 10:10 the liner was parallel to the pier and at 10:28 she was secured ready for gangways to be put in place.

VOYAGE 103 Eastbound and Westbound New York to Le Havre to Southampton to Bremerhaven to Le Havre to New York, 9 February to 24 February 1957.

VOYAGE 104 Eastbound and Westbound New York to Le Havre to Southampton to Bremerhaven to Le Havre to New York, 27 February to 13 March 1957.

VOYAGE 105 Eastbound and Westbound New York to Le Havre to Southampton to Bremerhaven to Le Havre to New York, 15 March to 29 March 1957.

Lord Beaverbrook, the famed British newspaper chain owner, was a first-class passenger on this voyage.

VOYAGE 106 Eastbound and Westbound New York to Le Havre to Southampton to Bremerhaven to Le Havre to Southampton to New York, 2 April to 16 April 1957.

VOYAGE 107 Eastbound and Westbound New York to Le Havre to Southampton to Le Havre to New York, 18 April to 29 April 1957.

VOYAGE 108 Eastbound and Westbound New York to Le Havre to Southampton to Le Havre to New York, 3 May to 14 May 1957.

VOYAGE 109 Eastbound and Westbound New York to Le Havre to Southampton to Le Havre to New York, 17 May to 28 May 1957.

VOYAGE 110 Eastbound and Westbound New York to Le Havre to Southampton to Le Havre to New York, 1 June to 12 June 1957.

4 June A report from Lookouts Swann and Barnes was received that the SS *United States* struck a whale. The vessel was inspected by divers at Le Havre and they confirmed no damage was discovered to the hull, rudder or propellers.

VOYAGE 111 Eastbound and Westbound New York to Le Havre to Southampton to Le Havre to New York, 14 June to 25 June 1957.

VOYAGE 112 Eastbound and Westbound New York to Le Havre to Southampton to Le Havre to New York, 28 June to 9 July 1957.

VOYAGE 113 Eastbound and Westbound New York to Le Havre to Southampton to Cherbourg to New York, 12 July to 23 July 1957.

18 July The SS *United States* was diverted to Cherbourg owing to an industrial dispute at Le Havre.

VOYAGE 114 Eastbound and Westbound New York to Le Havre to Southampton to Le Havre to New York, 25 July to 5 August 1957.

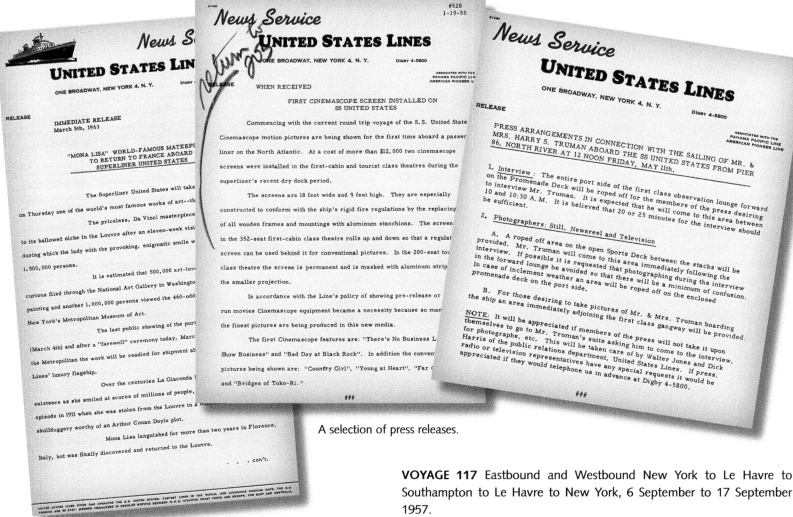

A selection of press releases.

The vessel departed from Pier 86, New York, at 16:03 on 5 August and arrived at Bayonne Dry Dock at 17:52 on 5 August. The ship departed from Bayonne Dry Dock at 07:00 on 8 August and returned to Pier 86, New York, at 08:54 on 8 August 1957.

VOYAGE 115 Eastbound and Westbound New York to Le Havre to Southampton to Le Havre to New York, 10 August to 21 August 1957.

VOYAGE 116 Eastbound and Westbound New York to Le Havre to Southampton to Le Havre to New York, 23 August to 3 September 1957.

VOYAGE 117 Eastbound and Westbound New York to Le Havre to Southampton to Le Havre to New York, 6 September to 17 September 1957.

VOYAGE 118 Eastbound and Westbound New York to Le Havre to Southampton to Le Havre to New York, 19 September to 30 September 1957.

21 September An emergency call was received from the US Coast Guard Cutter *Ingham* stating that a seaman aboard had been taken seriously ill with appendicitis. The SS *United States* diverted course to rendezvous with the USCGC *Ingham* and the casualty, named Stephen Long, was transferred to undergo an immediate appendectomy operation performed by the chief surgeon. The SS *United States* stopped at 17:09 until 17:54. Full speed was resumed at 18:14.

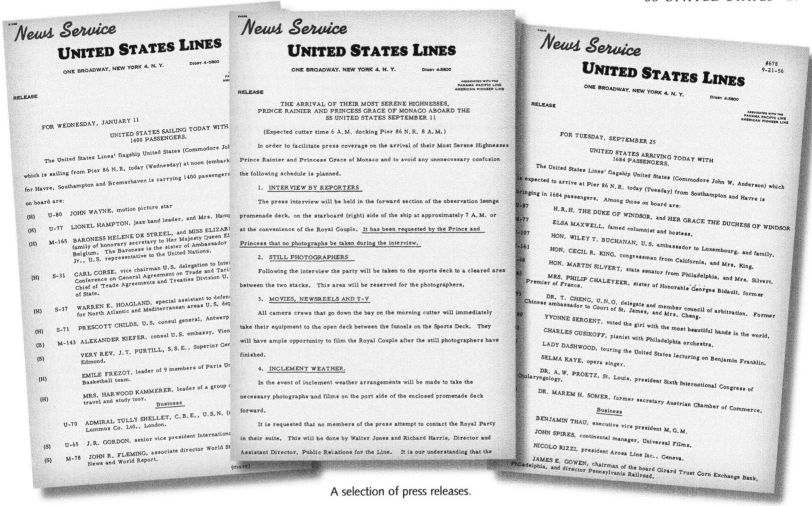

A selection of press releases.

VOYAGE 119 Eastbound and Westbound New York to Le Havre to Southampton to Le Havre to New York, 4 October to 15 October 1957.

VOYAGE 120 Eastbound and Westbound New York to Le Havre to Southampton to Le Havre to New York, 18 October to 29 October 1957.

VOYAGE 121 Eastbound and Westbound New York to Le Havre to Southampton to Bremerhaven to Le Havre to New York, 31 October to 14 November 1957.

VOYAGE 122 Eastbound and Westbound New York to Le Havre to Southampton to Bremerhaven to Le Havre to New York, 19 November to 3 December 1957.

VOYAGE 123 Eastbound and Westbound New York to Cherbourg to Southampton to Bremerhaven to Le Havre to New York, 6 December to 20 December 1957.

The ship departed from Pier 86, New York, at 17:05 on 20 December and arrived at Newport News Dry Dock at 06:46 on 21 December. On completion of work she departed from Newport News Dry Dock at 15:06 on 8 January 1958 returning to Pier 86, New York, at 05:28 on 9 January 1958.

VOYAGE 124 Eastbound and Westbound New York to Le Havre to Southampton to Bremerhaven to Le Havre to New York, 16 January to 30 January 1958.

VOYAGE 125 Eastbound and Westbound New York to Le Havre to Southampton to Bremerhaven to Le Havre to New York, 4 February to 18 February 1958.

The docking of the SS *United States* was delayed by heavy snow and ice in the Hudson and at Pier 86. All hands were advised to take extreme care and proceed with caution whilst on deck.

VOYAGE 126 Eastbound and Westbound New York to Le Havre to Southampton to Bremerhaven to Le Havre to New York, 21 February to 7 March 1958.

VOYAGE 127 Eastbound and Westbound New York to Le Havre to Southampton to Bremerhaven to Le Havre to New York, 11 March to 25 March 1958.

VOYAGE 128 Eastbound and Westbound New York to Le Havre to Southampton to Bremerhaven to Le Havre to New York, 27 March to 10 April 1958.

> **2 April** The logbook recorded 40ft-high seas and reduced speed delayed the arrival of the SS *United States* at Southampton by 24 hours.

VOYAGE 129 Eastbound and Westbound New York to Le Havre to Southampton to Le Havre to New York, 15 April to 29 April 1957.

VOYAGE 130 Eastbound and Westbound New York to Le Havre to Southampton to Le Havre to New York, 2 May to 13 May 1958.

VOYAGE 131 Eastbound and Westbound New York to Le Havre to Southampton to Le Havre to New York, 16 May to 27 May 1958.

VOYAGE 132 Eastbound and Westbound New York to Le Havre to Southampton to Le Havre to New York, 29 May to 9 June 1958.

VOYAGE 133 Eastbound and Westbound New York to Le Havre to Southampton to Le Havre to New York, 12 June to 23 June 1958.

VOYAGE 134 Eastbound and Westbound New York to Le Havre to Southampton to Le Havre to New York, 27 June to 8 July 1958.

VOYAGE 135 Eastbound and Westbound New York to Le Havre to Southampton to Le Havre to Southampton to New York, 10 July to 21 July 1958.

The vessel departed from Pier 86, New York, at 17:01 on 21 July and arrived at Bayonne Naval Ship Yard at 18:48 on 21 July 1958. With all work completed she departed from Bayonne Naval Ship Yard at 05:19 on 24 July and returned to Pier 86, New York, at 07:22 on 24 July 1958.

VOYAGE 136 Eastbound and Westbound New York to Le Havre to Southampton to Le Havre to New York, 26 July to 6 August 1958.

VOYAGE 137 Eastbound and Westbound New York to Le Havre to Southampton to Le Havre to New York, 8 August to 19 August 1958.

VOYAGE 138 Eastbound and Westbound New York to Le Havre to Southampton to Le Havre to New York, 22 August to 2 September 1958.

> **2 September** At 08:17 the aft lookouts reported a near-miss collision incident: whilst approaching Pier 86 with the SS *United States* during the 180-degree turning manoeuvre, the Cunard RMS *Queen Mary* passed within 30ft of the stern of the ship.

VOYAGE 139 Eastbound and Westbound New York to Le Havre to Southampton to Le Havre to New York, 5 September to 16 September 1958.

VOYAGE 140 Eastbound and Westbound New York to Le Havre to Southampton to Le Havre to New York, 19 September to 30 September 1958.

Proposed voyage for 1 October to 15 October cancelled owing to industrial action in New York. The vessel remained at idle status at Pier 86.

VOYAGE 141 Eastbound and Westbound New York to Le Havre to Southampton to Bremerhaven to Southampton to Le Havre to New York, 16 October to 30 October 1958.

VOYAGE 142 Eastbound and Westbound New York to Le Havre to Southampton to Bremerhaven to Southampton to Le Havre to New York, 1 November to 15 November 1958.

The VIP passenger list on board included Greer Garson and Merle Oberon.

13 November Whilst heading west from Le Havre at 32 knots at 08:13, the officer of the watch observed a passenger pacing the tourist-class outer deck when he suddenly jumped overboard. Quartermaster Barton threw a life-ring overboard. The order was given to reduce all engines to harbour speed at 85rpm, with a turn to starboard at 08:16. The engines were ordered to stop at 08:22, but with the momentum of the ship a 180-degree turn was achieved. Two minutes later at 08:24 the logbook records that it was safe to engage the engine at half astern, stopping again at 08:26, when the vessel came to a stop in the water. No.4 motor lifeboat was lowered with Dr Sheedy aboard to recover the passenger and guided in to position via signals from the ship's whistles (one blast to go to starboard, two blasts to port and three blasts to stern). The passenger, identified as a seventy-eight-year-old man named David Benzaria, was found dead after jumping 60ft from deck height to the sea.

Normally it would take the SS *United States* up to 20 minutes to come to a stop at 32 knots, but remarkably with this emergency she safely came to a halt in just under 10 minutes.

VOYAGE 143 Eastbound and Westbound New York to Le Havre to Southampton to Bremerhaven to Southampton to Le Havre to New York, 18 November to 5 December 1958.

VOYAGE 144 Eastbound and Westbound New York to Le Havre to Southampton to Bremerhaven to Southampton to Le Havre to New York, 10 December to 19 December 1958.
The ship departed from Pier 86, New York, at 20:08 on 19 December and arrived at Newport News Dry Dock at 09:43 on 20 December 1958. With all scheduled work completed she departed from Newport News Dry Dock at 19:08 on 7 January and arrived at Pier 86, New York, at 05:26 on 8 January 1959.

VOYAGE 145 Eastbound and Westbound New York to Le Havre to Southampton to Bremerhaven to Southampton to Le Havre to New York, 16 January to 30 January 1959.

VOYAGE 146 Eastbound and Westbound New York to Le Havre to Southampton to Bremerhaven to Southampton to Le Havre to New York, 3 February to 17 February 1959.

12 February Complaints were received from the tourist class that damage had been sustained to their clothing which had been taken by a bell boy for washing and pressing. Further complaints were received passengers Miss Geroa Rosenwald and Mr H. Azadecanian about slashes to material in their clothing. An investigation conducted by the Purser revealed that the Bell Boy had been storing garments and clothing in Locker 43 opposite the Chief Steward's Office while awaiting delivery to the valet. The use of this temporary locker was discontinued and all damages paid for by United States Lines as compensation.

A covering of heavy snow and thick ice on the Hudson delayed arrival of the SS *United States*.

VOYAGE 147 Eastbound and Westbound New York to Le Havre to Southampton to Bremerhaven to Southampton to Le Havre to New York, 19 February to 4 March 1959.

VOYAGE 148 Eastbound and Westbound New York to Le Havre to Southampton to Bremerhaven to Southampton to Le Havre to New York, 6 March to 20 March 1959.

VOYAGE 149 Eastbound and Westbound New York to Le Havre to Southampton to Bremerhaven to Southampton to Le Havre to New York, 24 March to 7 April 1959.

25 March A stowaway was apprehended in a lifeboat and taken to the ship's brig for secure detention.

26 March At 04:00, passengers in the tourist class room D59 complained about banging noises and calls for help. Mr Suissa, tourist assistant chief purser, investigated and reported that the disturbance originated from the stowaway. The passengers were informed of the situation and told that remediable action would be taken. The Master at Arms was summoned to 'forcibly quieten down' the stowaway.

VOYAGE 150 Eastbound and Westbound New York to Le Havre to Southampton to Bremerhaven to Southampton to Le Havre to New York, 9 April to 22 April 1959.

VOYAGE 151 Eastbound and Westbound New York to Le Havre to Southampton to Le Havre to New York, 24 April to 5 May 1959.

VOYAGE 152 Eastbound and Westbound New York to Le Havre to Southampton to Le Havre to New York, 8 May to 19 May 1959.

VOYAGE 153 Eastbound and Westbound New York to Le Havre to Southampton to Le Havre to New York, 22 May to 2 June 1959.

VOYAGE 154 Eastbound and Westbound New York to Le Havre to Southampton to Le Havre to New York, 4 June to 15 June 1959.

VOYAGE 155 Eastbound and Westbound New York to Le Havre to Southampton to Le Havre to New York, 19 June to 30 June 1959.

VOYAGE 156 Eastbound and Westbound New York to Le Havre to Southampton to Le Havre to New York, 2 July to 13 July 1959.

VOYAGE 157 Eastbound and Westbound New York to Le Havre to Southampton to Le Havre to New York, 16 July to 27 July 1959.

The ship departed from Pier 86, New York, at 16:59 and arrived at Bayonne Naval Dock at 18:41 on 27 July. With all scheduled work completed she departed from Bayonne Naval Dock at 05:11 and returned to Pier 86, New York, at 07:11 on 30 July 1959.

VOYAGE 158 Eastbound and Westbound New York to Le Havre to Southampton to Le Havre to New York, 31 July to 11 August 1959.

VOYAGE 159 Eastbound and Westbound New York to Le Havre to Southampton to Le Havre to New York, 14 August to 25 August 1959.

VOYAGE 160 Eastbound and Westbound New York to Le Havre to Southampton to Le Havre to New York, 28 August to 8 September 1959.

VOYAGE 161 Eastbound and Westbound New York to Le Havre to Southampton to Le Havre to New York, 11 September to 22 September 1959.

VOYAGE 162 Eastbound and Westbound New York to Le Havre to Southampton to Le Havre to New York, 25 September to 6 October 1959.

VOYAGE 163 Eastbound and Westbound New York to Le Havre to Southampton to Le Havre to New York, 8 October to 19 October 1959.

VOYAGE 164 Eastbound and Westbound New York to Le Havre to Southampton to Bremerhaven to Southampton to Le Havre to New York, 22 October to 4 November 1959.

VOYAGE 165 Eastbound and Westbound New York to Le Havre to Southampton to Bremerhaven to Southampton to Le Havre to New York, 6 November to 20 November 1959.

VOYAGE 166 Eastbound and Westbound New York to Le Havre to Southampton to Bremerhaven to Southampton to Le Havre to New York, 24 November to 7 December 1959.

VOYAGE 167 Eastbound and Westbound New York to Le Havre to Southampton to Bremerhaven to Southampton to Le Havre to New York, 9 December to 22 December 1959.

The ship departed from Pier 86, New York, at 03:32 on 23 December and arrived at Newport News Dry Dock at 12:30 on 23 December 1959. With all scheduled work completed she departed from Newport News Dry Dock at 19:34 on 7 January and returned to Pier 86, New York, at 05:09 on 8 January 1960.

VOYAGE 168 Eastbound and Westbound New York to Le Havre to Southampton to Bremerhaven to Southampton to Le Havre to New York, 12 January to 25 January 1960.

VOYAGE 169 Eastbound and Westbound New York to Le Havre to Southampton to Bremerhaven to Southampton to Le Havre to New York, 27 January to 9 February 1960.

VOYAGE 170 Eastbound and Westbound New York to Cherbourg to Southampton to Bremerhaven to Southampton to Le Havre to New York, 11 February to 24 February 1960.

VOYAGE 171 Eastbound and Westbound New York to Le Havre to Southampton to Bremerhaven to Southampton to Le Havre to New York, 26 February to 10 March 1960.

VOYAGE 172 Eastbound and Westbound New York to Le Havre to Southampton to Bremerhaven to Southampton to Le Havre to New York, 12 March to 25 March 1960.

VOYAGE 173 Eastbound and Westbound New York to Le Havre to Southampton to Bremerhaven to Southampton to Le Havre to New York, 29 March to 11 April 1960.

VOYAGE 174 Eastbound and Westbound New York to Le Havre to Southampton to Le Havre to New York, 14 April to 25 April 1960.

VOYAGE 175 Eastbound and Westbound New York to Le Havre to Southampton to Bremerhaven to Southampton to Le Havre to New York, 27April to 10 May 1960.

VOYAGE 176 Eastbound and Westbound New York to Le Havre to Southampton to Le Havre to New York, 12 May to 23 May 1960.

VOYAGE 177 Eastbound and Westbound New York to Le Havre to Southampton to Le Havre to New York, 26 May to 6 June 1960.

VOYAGE 178 Eastbound and Westbound New York to Le Havre to Southampton to Le Havre to New York, 9 June to 20 June 1960.

VOYAGE 179 Eastbound and Westbound New York to Le Havre to Southampton to Le Havre to New York, 24 June to 5 July 1960.

VOYAGE 180 Eastbound and Westbound New York to Le Havre to Southampton to Le Havre to New York, 8 July to 19 July 1960.

VOYAGE 181 Eastbound and Westbound New York to Le Havre to Southampton to Le Havre to New York, 21 July to 1 August 1960.

VOYAGE 182 Eastbound and Westbound New York to Le Havre to Southampton to Le Havre to New York, 5 August to 16 August 1960.

VOYAGE 183 Eastbound and Westbound New York to Le Havre to Southampton to Le Havre to New York, 18 August to 29 August 1960.

VOYAGE 184 Eastbound and Westbound New York to Le Havre to Southampton to Le Havre to New York, 1 September to 12 September 1960.

VOYAGE 185 Eastbound and Westbound New York to Le Havre to Southampton to Le Havre to New York, 15 September to 26 September 1960.

VOYAGE 186 Eastbound and Westbound New York to Le Havre to Southampton to Le Havre to New York, 28 September to 9 October 1960.

VOYAGE 187 Eastbound and Westbound New York to Le Havre to Southampton to Le Havre to New York, 11 October to 22 October 1960.

VOYAGE 188 Eastbound and Westbound New York to Le Havre to Southampton to Bremerhaven to Southampton to Le Havre to New York, 25 October to 7 November 1960.

28 October Approaching the port of Southampton, the Chief Purser reported that the crew safe on A Deck in the purser's office had been robbed and that approximately $40,000 of the crew wages was missing! This information was radioed ahead to the company's office at Southampton. After docking, United States Line officials boarded the ship with two City of Southampton Constabulary CID police officers. A thorough search was conducted and the crew was questioned at length with no success or recovery of the missing cash.

The investigation continued in New York with FBI agents interviewing the crew and a search was conducted by forty-one officers of the Customs Service, again with no success. In early February 1961, it came to light that a bell boy had opened the safe and removed the cash, taken it ashore at Le Havre and hidden it in a park. Unfortunately, the majority of the cash in notes had been partially destroyed owing to rain and snow. The boy was subsequently arrested by the US Federal Authority.

VOYAGE 189 Eastbound and Westbound New York to Le Havre to Southampton to Bremerhaven to Southampton to Le Havre to New York, 9 November to 22 November 1960.

VOYAGE 190 Eastbound and Westbound New York to Le Havre to Southampton to Bremerhaven to Southampton to Le Havre to New York, 25 November to 9 December 1960.

The SS United States arrived at Pier 86 some 24 hours late following a delayed departure from Le Havre. The quick turnaround for Voyage 191 was achieved by 350 longshoremen in 28 hours instead of the normal 52 hours.

VOYAGE 191 Eastbound and Westbound New York to Le Havre to Southampton to Le Havre to New York, 10 to 21 December 1960.

A selection of menus from the
SS *United States*.

Jumbo Shrimp Cocktail   Pâté de Foie Gras   Fresh Crabmeat Cocktail
Chilled Spanish Melon   Filet of Matjes Herring in Wine Sauce
Iced Table Celery   Queen Olives

* * *

Green Turtle, "Windsor" en Tasse   Cream of Mushrooms

* * *

Broiled Pompano, Mushroom Butter, Saratoga Chips
Spanish Scampi à la Provençale, Saffron Risotto

* * *

Roast: Stuffed Cornish Rock Game Hen, Giblet Sauce, Cranberry Jelly
Baked Sugar-cured Ham, Sauce Burgundy

* * *

From the Grill: Bone-in Sirloin Steak, Fresh Mushrooms, Sauté

* * *

Corn on the Cob, Melted Butter
Cauliflower au Gratin   Petits Pois
Haricots Verts
Potatoes: Boiled, Baked Idaho, French Fried or Candied Sweet

* * *

Chef's Salad Bowl, Special or Roquefort Dressing

* * *

Preserved Royal Anne Cherries

* * *

Vienna Mocha Layer Cake   Butter Pecan Ice Cream, Chocolate Sauce

* * *

Swiss, Gorgonzola or Neufchâtel Cheese and Toasted Crackers

* * *

Crystallized Ginger   Assorted Nuts   After Dinner Mints
California Figs   Tunis Dates

* * *

Fresh Fruit in Season

* * *

Coffee   Tea   Fresh Milk

EB—TCD-IV   Monday, June 4, 1962

Chilled Spanish Melon
Suprême of Fresh Fruit in Kirschwasser   Crabmeat Cocktail
Chopped Chicken Liver, Garni   Smoked Irish Salmon
Jumbo Shrimp Cocktail   Pâté de Foie Gras Truffé
Iced Table Celery   Ripe and Queen Olives

* * *

Kangaroo Tail Soup   Fresh Green Turtle, Windsor   Velouté Bismarck

* * *

Spanish Scampi à la Provençale en Casserole, Saffron Risotto
Poached Filet of Sole, "Bonne-Femme"

* * *

Chukkar Partridge, Strasbourgeoise
Champagne Kraut, Foie Gras, Sour Cream Sauce

* * *

Chartreuse Sherbet, Nabisco Wafers

* * *

Roast Stuffed Philadelphia Capon, Giblet Sauce, Cranberry Jelly
Roast Southdown Lamb au Jus, Mint Jelly

* * *

Prime Sirloin Steak, Mushrooms, Sauté, Sauce Béarnaise

* * *

California Asparagus, Melted Butter
Petits Pois à la Française Fresh String Beans, Sauté Zucchini Squash, Sauté
Parsley, Mousseline, Baked Idaho or French Fried Potatoes

* * *

Avocado Pear, French Dressing

* * *

Preserved Royal Anne Cherries

* * *

Bombe Glacée, Mignon   Petits Fours

* * *

Swiss, Gorgonzola or Stilton Cheese and Toasted Crackers

* * *

Crystallized Ginger   Assorted Nuts   After Dinner Mints
Table Figs   Tunis Dates

* * *

Fresh Fruit Basket

* * *

Demi Tasse

WB—CCD-V   Monday, May 8, 1961

Captain's Dinner

•

Beluga Malossol Caviar on Ice
Chilled Fresh Fruit Cup in Kirschwasser
Cape Cod Oysters on the Half Shell   Smoked Irish Salmon
Iced Table Celery   Pâté de Foie Gras aux Truffles
Queen and Ripe Olives

Creme Alexandria

Clear Green Turtle Soup Windsor
Cold: Jellied Madrilene

Poached Darne of Kennebec Salmon, Dieppoise
Fresh Brook Trout Sauté Meuniere, Waldorf Salad

Braised Sweetbread Financiere

Refreshment: Champagne Sherbet, Nabisco Wafers

Roast Philadelphia Capon, Chestnut Dressing, Giblet Sauce, Cranberry Jelly
Roast Saddle of Spring Lamb, Mint Jelly
From the Grill: Filet Mignon, Parisienne, Sauce Bercy

Compote: Preserved Royale Anne Cherries

Garden Broccoli Hollandaise
Green String Beans Sauté
Potatoes: Parsley, Mousseline, French Fried, Baked Idaho or Fondante   Petits Pois à la Française

Avocado Salad, Special Dressing

Bombe Glace Mignon   Gateau Noisette   Mignardises

Assorted Cheese and Toasted Crackers

Assorted Nuts
Tunis Dates   After Dinner Mints   Table Raisins
Crystallized Ginger   Table Figs
Fresh Fruit Basket   Grapes on Ice

Demi Tasse

EB-FC-Capt.-Din 6   Sunday, December 20, 1953

The ship departed from Pier 86, New York, at 17:00 on 21 December and arrived at Newport News Dry Dock Shipway No.11 at 09:00 on 22 December 1960. She departed from Newport News Dry Dock Shipway No.11 at 12:00 and arrived at Newport News Shipyard Dock 10 at 13:39 on 5 January 1961. The vessel departed from Newport News Shipyard Dock 10 at 14:21 on 7 January 1961 and returned to Pier 86, New York, at 08:30 on 8 January 1961.

VOYAGE 192 Eastbound and Westbound New York to Le Havre to Southampton to Bremerhaven to Southampton to Le Havre to New York, 10 January to 24 January 1961.

VOYAGE 193 Eastbound and Westbound New York to Le Havre to Southampton to Bremerhaven to Southampton to Le Havre to New York, 26 January to 8 February 1961.

27 January, 08:00 to 20:00 The logbook recorded the vessel encrusted with ice which caused two main deck doors to be buckled. Weather was described as overcast with heavy snow squalls. The 75mph winds caused 60ft-high waves, forcing the ship to reduce speed.

28 January The vessel was recorded rolling 12 degrees starboard and 10 degrees port in rough WNW sea.

29 January, 04:00 to 08:00 The ship was logged rolling 15 degrees to port and 13 degrees to starboard in rough WNW sea. Passenger complaints

8 March Following departure from Cherbourg, off the west coast of Ireland, the vessel entered a storm with winds coming from a NNE direction at Force 6 at 02:00. By 12:00 the logbook reported that the storm had increased to Force 8 with a change in direction of the wind from the SE. This resulted in the SS *United States* rolling 12 degrees to port and starboard. The weather continued to deteriorate with wind direction switching to the north. The ship passed through snow and freezing rain squalls with the vessel now alarmingly recorded rolling at 22 degrees to port and 12 degrees to starboard in very rough northerly sea swells with spray breaking over the decks, although speed was reduced to 120rpm on the propellers. A further reduction in speed to just 75rpm was ordered at 02:55 to bring the ship down to 10 knots. No major injuries reported by passengers or crew, only cuts and bruises.

VOYAGE 196 Eastbound and Westbound New York to Le Havre to Southampton to Bremerhaven to Southampton to Le Havre to New York, 14 March to 27 March 1961.

VOYAGE 197 Eastbound and Westbound New York to Le Havre to Southampton to Bremerhaven to Southampton to Le Havre to New York, 29 March to 12 April 1961.

VOYAGE 198 Eastbound and Westbound New York to Le Havre to Southampton to Le Havre to New York, 14 April to 25 April 1961.

VOYAGE 199 Eastbound and Westbound New York to Le Havre to Southampton to Bremerhaven to Southampton to Le Havre to New York, 27 April to 10 May 1961.

VOYAGE 200 Eastbound and Westbound New York to Le Havre to Southampton to Le Havre to New York, 12 May to 23 May 1961.

VOYAGE 201 Eastbound and Westbound New York to Le Havre to Southampton to Le Havre to New York, 25 May to 5 June 1961.

VOYAGE 202 Eastbound and Westbound New York to Le Havre to Southampton to Bremerhaven to Southampton to Le Havre to New York, 8 June to 21 June 1961.

20 June, 14:25 A distress call was received from the MV *Atlantic Duke* to pick up a badly injured seaman, Gerontakis Stavros, pumpman.

recorded in the log of vessel due to vibration and sea sickness. Captain John Anderson entered into the log, 'This is her worst crossing yet.'

VOYAGE 194 Eastbound and Westbound New York to Le Havre to Southampton to Bremerhaven to Southampton to Le Havre to New York, 10 February to 24 February 1961.

VOYAGE 195 Eastbound and Westbound New York to Le Havre to Southampton to Bremerhaven to Southampton to Cherbourg to New York, 25 February to 10 March 1961.

14:27 A reverse course was plotted on the bridge and new course set to intercept the MV *Atlantic* with speed increased to 155rpm to 33 knots. At 17:20 the MV *Atlantic* was sighted 5 degrees on the port bow. The order to reduce speed to half ahead was made at 17:56 and manoeuvre to make an approach, opening the starboard forward stores port boat deck door. At 18:05 the SS *United States* was stopped. By 18:19 the MV *Atlantic*'s lifeboat was alongside and at 18:24 the stretcher was hoisted aboard. The lifeboat was away at 18:26. With the stores port closed and order given full ahead to New York at 18:28, increasing speed to 150rpm at the propellers to achieve 33 knots. Upon arrival at New York on 21 June, the injured seaman was given priority disembarkation and transported to the Marine Hospital at 14:30 by ambulance.

21 June When the SS *United States* docked at Pier 86, there was a strike. Passengers were allowed to disembark, but no cargo was unloaded.

VOYAGE 203 Idle Status New York, 23 June to 4 July 1961.
Owing to industrial action the planned voyages starting on 24 June with 1,731 bookings and 1 July with 1,325 bookings were cancelled. One boiler was kept in steam and the diesel emergency generator used for lighting and power on board. The bilges were pumped out routinely and the refrigeration system maintained to preserve all frozen food stocks.

VOYAGE 204 Eastbound and Westbound New York to Le Havre to Southampton to Le Havre to New York, 6 July to 18 July 1961.
The SS *United States* sailed with unloaded cargo brought in on 21 June due to industrial action.

VOYAGE 205 Eastbound and Westbound New York to Le Havre to Southampton to Le Havre to New York, 20 July to 31 July 1961.

VOYAGE 206 Eastbound and Westbound New York to Le Havre to Southampton to Le Havre to New York, 4 August to 15 August 1961.

VOYAGE 207 Eastbound and Westbound New York to Le Havre to Southampton to Le Havre to New York, 17 August to 28 August 1961.
A Walt Disney film crew was present aboard the SS *United States* to film location sequences for the film, *Bon Voyage*. The film stars present were Jane Wyman, Fred MacMurray, Michael Callan, Deborah Wally, Tommy Kirk, Kevin Corcoran and Anna Maria Majalca. Walt Disney himself accompanied film producer William Walsh on the voyage across the Atlantic. During the departure of the liner from New York, film crews recorded the scene from Pier 86, a second crew filmed from a helicopter above and the third from the ship. With the active co-operation of Commodore Anderson of the SS *United States*, the ship travelled at only half-ahead speed for the first 75 miles out of New York while a film crew shot action shots of the SS *United States* at sea taken from a Coast Guard cutter.

VOYAGE 208 Eastbound and Westbound New York to Le Havre to Southampton to Le Havre to New York, 31 August to 11 September 1961.

VOYAGE 209 Eastbound and Westbound New York to Le Havre to Southampton to Le Havre to New York, 14 September to 25 September 1961.

VOYAGE 210 Eastbound and Westbound New York to Le Havre to Southampton to Le Havre to New York, 28 September to 9 October 1961.

29 September A stowaway apprehended and detained in custody in the brig awaiting transfer to the police upon arrival at New York.

VOYAGE 211 Eastbound and Westbound New York to Le Havre to Southampton to Bremerhaven to Southampton to Le Havre to New York, 10 October to 22 October 1961.

VOYAGE 212 Eastbound and Westbound New York to Le Havre to Southampton to Bremerhaven to Southampton to Le Havre to New York, 23 October to 6 November 1961.
President Tubman of Liberia was amongst the VIPs on board.

VOYAGE 213 Eastbound and Westbound New York to Le Havre to Southampton to Le Havre to New York, 8 November to 21 November 1961.
The ship departed from Pier 86, New York, at 16:00 on 21 November and arrived at Newport News Dry Dock at 07:36 on 22 November 1961. The vessel departed Newport News Dry Dock at 16:00 on 5 November 1961, returning to Pier 86, New York, at 07:45 on 6 December 1961.

VOYAGE 214 Eastbound and Westbound New York to Le Havre to Southampton to Bremerhaven to Southampton to Le Havre to New York, 9 December to 22 December 1961.

VOYAGE 215 Eastbound and Westbound New York to Le Havre to Southampton to Bremerhaven to Southampton to Le Havre to New York, 28 December 1961 to 10 January 1962.

VOYAGE 216 Eastbound and Westbound New York to Le Havre to Southampton to Bremerhaven to Southampton to Le Havre to New York, 13 January to 27 January 1962.

VOYAGE 217 Cruise: New York to Nassau to St Thomas to Dragon's Mouth to Port of Spain anchorage to Caracas Bay Berth to Cristóbal to New York, 30 January to 13 February 1962.

VOYAGE 218 Cruise: New York to Nassau to St Thomas to Dragon's Mouth to Port of Spain anchorage to Caracas Bay Berth to Cristóbal to New York, 16 February to 2 March 1962.

VOYAGE 219 Eastbound and Westbound New York to Le Havre to Southampton to Bremerhaven to Southampton to Le Havre to New York, 6 March to 20 March 1962.

6 March, 14:47 Whilst outbound from New York, the SS *United States* was stopped just past the Gedney buoy at the entrance to New York Harbour in order to disembark the Sandy Hook pilot, Captain Harold Kaiser. At 14:52 the starboard pilot port door was opened. With the vessel pitching and rolling heavily in high NNE sea, the starboard pilot port submerged underwater causing flooding of the adjacent passageway and staterooms. A further attempt was made to disembark the pilot, but the transfer was cancelled at 15:00 and the pilot port door closed. The unexpected guest was dried off, reclothed and made welcome for the voyage across the Atlantic.

VOYAGE 220 Eastbound and Westbound New York to Le Havre to Southampton to Bremerhaven to Southampton to Le Havre to New York, 21 March to 3 April 1962.

VOYAGE 221 Eastbound and Westbound New York to Le Havre to Southampton to Bremerhaven to Southampton to Le Havre to New York, 6 April to 19 April 1962.

VOYAGE 222 Eastbound and Westbound New York to Le Havre to Southampton to Le Havre to New York, 21 April to 2 May 1962.

VOYAGE 223 Eastbound and Westbound New York to Le Havre to Southampton to Le Havre to New York, 5 May to 16 May 1962.

VOYAGE 224 Eastbound and Westbound New York to Le Havre to Southampton to Le Havre to New York, 18 May to 29 May 1962.

VOYAGE 225 Eastbound and Westbound New York to Le Havre to Southampton to Le Havre to New York, 1 June to 12 June 1962.

VOYAGE 226 Eastbound and Westbound New York to Le Havre to Southampton to Bremerhaven to Southampton to Le Havre to New York, 14 June to 27 June 1962.

VOYAGE 227 Eastbound and Westbound New York to Le Havre to Southampton to Le Havre to New York, 29 June to 10 July 1962.

8 July, 15:45 An urgent distress call was received from the British yacht, *Ramona C.*, requesting to pick up Captain Richard Hughes following injuries suffered from a swinging boom. The SS *United States* immediately diverted from Tack C westbound to Lat. 43 degrees, 11 minutes north, 150 miles off course at an increased speed of 35 knots. At 20:25 the yacht was spotted on the radar and speed was reduced to half ahead at 20:51. The SS *United States* was stopped at 21:15 and motor lifeboat No.3 was lowered to recover Captain Hughes. The injured man was received on board at 22:06 through the starboard stores port and with the lifeboat retrieved at 22:16, full steam ahead resumed a minute later.

VOYAGE 228 Eastbound and Westbound New York to Le Havre to Southampton to Le Havre to New York, 12 July to 23 July 1962.

VOYAGE 229 Eastbound and Westbound New York to Le Havre to Southampton to Le Havre to New York, 27 July to 7 August 1962.

VOYAGE 230 Eastbound and Westbound New York to Le Havre to Southampton to Bremerhaven to Southampton to Le Havre to New York, 9 August to 22 August 1962.

VOYAGE 231 Eastbound and Westbound New York to Le Havre to Southampton to Le Havre to New York, 25 August to 5 September 1962.

VOYAGE 232 Eastbound and Westbound New York to Le Havre to Southampton to Le Havre to New York, 7 September to 18 September 1962.

VOYAGE 233 Eastbound and Westbound New York to Le Havre to Southampton to Le Havre to New York, 21 September to 2 October 1962.

VOYAGE 234 Logbook states, 'Vessel Strikebound. No ship's crew aboard.'

VOYAGE 235 Eastbound and Westbound New York to Le Havre to Southampton to Le Havre to New York, 19 October to 30 October 1962.

VOYAGE 236 Eastbound and Westbound New York to Le Havre to Southampton to Bremerhaven to Southampton to Le Havre to New York, 2 November to 16 November 1962.

The ship departed from Pier 86, New York, at 16:01 on 15 November and arrived at Newport News Dry Dock at 08:40 on 16 November 1962. She departed from Newport News Dry Dock at 02:54 on 4 December and returned to Pier 86, New York, at 10:16 on 5 December 1962.

VOYAGE 237 Eastbound and Westbound New York to Le Havre to Southampton to Bremerhaven to Southampton to Le Havre to New York, 10 December to 23 December 1962.

Depart Pier 86, New York, at 14:34 on 23 December 1962.
Arrive Newport News Dry Dock at 09:03 on 24 December 1962.

VOYAGE 238 Logbook for Voyage 238 commences at Newport News Dry Dock.

Depart Newport News Dry Dock at 15:06 9 February 1963.
Arrive Pier 86, New York, at 08:23 on 10 February 1963.

VOYAGES 239 and 240 Cancelled – no logbooks available.

VOYAGE 241 Cruise: New York to Nassau to St Thomas to Curaçao to Martinique to Trinidad to Cristóbal to New York, 16 February to 4 March 1963.

VOYAGE 242 Eastbound and Westbound New York to Le Havre to Southampton to Bremerhaven to Southampton to Le Havre to New York, 7 March to 20 March 1963.

A three-room suite was reserved for guards from the Louvre Gallery in Paris, France, who were escorting the world-famous *Mona Lisa* painting, which was returning to France.

VOYAGE 243 Eastbound and Westbound New York to Le Havre to Southampton to Bremerhaven to Southampton to Le Havre to New York, 23 March to 5 April 1963.

VOYAGE 244 Eastbound and Westbound New York to Le Havre to Southampton to Bremerhaven to Southampton to Le Havre to New York, 9 April to 22 April 1963.

VOYAGE 245 Eastbound and Westbound New York to Le Havre to Southampton to Bremerhaven to Southampton to Le Havre to New York, 24 April to 7 May 1963.

VOYAGE 246 Eastbound and Westbound New York to Le Havre to Southampton to Bremerhaven to Southampton to Le Havre to New York, 10 May to 23 May 1963.

VOYAGE 247 Eastbound and Westbound New York to Le Havre to Southampton to Le Havre to New York, 25 May to 5 June 1963.

27 May A report was submitted from Montague Banks, junior assistant tourist class purser, regarding the swimming pool attendant and complaints of insolence to passengers and insubordination to the ship's officers. Complaints had been received from passengers Mrs Wartham and Mrs Gibson stating that their children had been prevented from entering the swimming pool without their parents. The pool attendant stated, 'I am the Commodore in this place.' When addressed by the junior purser, the pool attendant shouted, 'No God damn purser is going to give me orders'. The passengers were apologised to and the matter referred higher for disciplinary action.

VOYAGE 248 Eastbound and Westbound New York to Le Havre to Southampton to Le Havre to New York, 7 June to 18 June 1963.

VOYAGE 249 Eastbound and Westbound New York to Le Havre to Southampton to Le Havre to New York, 21 June to 2 July 1963.

VOYAGE 250 Eastbound and Westbound New York to Le Havre to Southampton to Le Havre to New York, 5 July to 16 July 1963.

VOYAGE 251 Eastbound and Westbound New York to Le Havre to Southampton to Le Havre to New York, 18 July to 29 July 1963.

VOYAGE 252 Eastbound and Westbound New York to Le Havre to Southampton to Bremerhaven to Southampton to Le Havre to New York, 2 August to 15 August 1963.

VOYAGE 253 Eastbound and Westbound New York to Le Havre to Southampton to Le Havre to New York, 17 August to 28 August 1963.

VOYAGE 254 Eastbound and Westbound New York to Le Havre to Southampton to Le Havre to New York, 30 August to 10 September 1963.

VOYAGE 255 Eastbound and Westbound New York to Le Havre to Southampton to Le Havre to New York, 13 September to 24 September 1963.

VOYAGE 256 Eastbound and Westbound New York to Le Havre to Southampton to Le Havre to New York, 27 September to 8 October 1963.

A complaint was received from Hollywood film star Rita Hayworth, who was a passenger on board in cabin M69, that her toilet seat had been stolen! Miss Hayworth alleged that it had been taken by a member of the crew as a souvenir. An investigation was undertaken by the chief purser, crew quarters searched but after further questioning the crew denied all knowledge of it and the seat was not recovered.

VOYAGE 257 Eastbound and Westbound New York to Le Havre to Southampton to Le Havre to New York, 10 October to 21 October 1963.

VOYAGE 258 Eastbound and Westbound New York to Le Havre to Southampton to Bremerhaven to Southampton to Le Havre to New York, 23 October to 5 November 1963.

VOYAGE 259 Eastbound and Westbound New York to Le Havre to Southampton to Bremerhaven to Southampton to Le Havre to New York, 7 November to 20 November 1963.

The ship departed from Pier 86, New York, at 17:56 on 21 November and arrived at Newport News Dry Dock at 05:06 on 22 November 1963. She departed from Newport News Dry Dock at 18:44 on 7 December and returned to Pier 86, New York, at 10:16 on 8 December 1963.

VOYAGE 260 Eastbound and Westbound New York to Le Havre to Southampton to Le Havre to New York, 12 December to 23 December 1963.

The logbook recorded that the SS *United States* was delayed by 21 hours owing to severe weather conditions with gale force 8 head winds. The ship entered the port of Southampton and was unloaded and turned around in just 6 hours, instead of the normal allocated 22 hours, in order to return to New York for Christmas.

VOYAGE 261 Cruise: New York to Curaçao to Martinique to St Thomas to New York, 27 December 1963 to 5 January 1964.

VOYAGE 262 Eastbound and Westbound New York to Le Havre to Southampton to Bremerhaven to Southampton to Le Havre to New York, 8 January to 21 January 1964.

VOYAGE 263 Eastbound and Westbound New York to Le Havre to Southampton to Bremerhaven to Southampton to Le Havre to New York, 23 January to 5 February 1964.

5 February The SS *United States* docked unassisted without tugs. During the docking manoeuvre a hawser snapped and the total delay was recorded as 5 hours.

VOYAGE 264 New York to Nassau to Curaçao to Martinique to St Thomas to New York, 8 February to 19 February 1964.

19 February Owing to industrial action, the SS *United States* docked again unaided without the assistance of tugs. The snow flurries and gusting winds slightly hampered docking.

VOYAGE 265 Eastbound and Westbound New York to Le Havre to Southampton to Bremerhaven to Southampton to Le Havre to New York, 22 February to 6 March 1964.

VOYAGE 266 Eastbound and Westbound New York to Le Havre to Southampton to Bremerhaven to Southampton to Le Havre to New York, 10 March to 23 March 1964.

The Duke and Duchess of Windsor were aboard travelling in the 'Duck Suite' with almost 100 items of luggage.

VOYAGE 267 New York to Bermuda (anchored in the Great Sound) to Martinique to St Thomas to Nassau to New York, 26 March to 5 April 1964.

VOYAGE 268 Eastbound and Westbound New York to Le Havre to Southampton to Bremerhaven to Southampton to Le Havre to New York, 7 April to 20 April 1964.

VOYAGE 269 Eastbound and Westbound New York to Le Havre to Southampton to Le Havre to New York, 23 April to 4 May 1964.

VOYAGE 270 Eastbound and Westbound New York to Le Havre to Southampton to Bremerhaven to Southampton to Le Havre to New York, 7 May to 20 May 1964.

VOYAGE 271 Eastbound and Westbound New York to Le Havre to Southampton to Le Havre to New York, 22 May to 2 June 1964.

VOYAGE 272 Eastbound and Westbound New York to Le Havre to Southampton to Bremerhaven to Southampton to Le Havre to New York, 5 June to 16 June 1964.

VOYAGE 273 Eastbound and Westbound New York to Le Havre to Southampton to Bremerhaven to Southampton to Le Havre to New York, 18 June to 1 July 1964.

VOYAGE 274 Eastbound and Westbound New York to Le Havre to Southampton to Le Havre to New York, 3 July to 14 July 1964.

VOYAGE 275 Eastbound and Westbound New York to Le Havre to Southampton to Le Havre to New York, 17 July to 28 July 1964.

VOYAGE 276 Eastbound and Westbound New York to Le Havre to Southampton to Le Havre to New York, 30 July to 10 August 1964.

VOYAGE 277 Eastbound and Westbound New York to Le Havre to Southampton to Le Havre to New York, 14 August to 25 August 1964.

VOYAGE 278 Eastbound and Westbound New York to Le Havre to Southampton to Le Havre to New York, 27 August to 7 September 1964.

VOYAGE 279 Eastbound and Westbound New York to Le Havre to Southampton to Le Havre to New York, 10 September to 21 September 1964.

VOYAGE 280 Eastbound and Westbound New York to Le Havre to Southampton to Le Havre to New York, 24 September to 5 October 1964.

VOYAGE 281 Eastbound and Westbound New York to Le Havre to Southampton to Le Havre to New York, 7 October to 18 October 1964.

VOYAGE 282 Eastbound and Westbound New York to Le Havre to Southampton to Bremerhaven to Southampton to Le Havre to New York, 20 October to 2 November 1964.

The ship departed from Pier 86, New York, at 16:07 on 2 November and arrived at Newport News Dry Dock at 05:50 on 3 November 1964. She departed from Newport News Dry Dock at 16:00 on 20 November and returned to Pier 86, New York, at 14:37 on 21 November 1964.

21 November The completed Verrazano Bridge was opened and the SS *United States* was the first vessel to officially sail under. A special commemorative first day postal cover was released for the occasion.

VOYAGE 283 Cruise: New York to Bermuda to New York, 25 November to 30 November 1964.

VOYAGE 284 Eastbound and Westbound New York to Le Havre to Southampton to Bremerhaven to Southampton to Le Havre to New York, 2 December to 15 December 1964.

VOYAGE 285 Cruise: New York to Curaçao to Martinique to St Thomas to New York, 18 December to 27 December 1964.

VOYAGE 286 Eastbound and Westbound New York to Le Havre to Southampton to Bremerhaven to Southampton to Le Havre to New York, 29 December 1964 to 11 January 1965.

VOYAGE 287 12 January to 27 January 1965. The logbook records that the vessel remained in port throughout, tied up at Pier 86.

16 January, 15:50 A British stowaway from Liverpool, Michael S. Thomas, was brought on board from the SS *American Press* and detained in custody in the ship's brig to await transfer.

VOYAGE 288 Eastbound and Westbound New York to Le Havre to Southampton to Bremerhaven to Southampton to Le Havre to New York, 29 January to 11 February 1965.

VOYAGE 289 Cruise: New York to Nassau to Curaçao to St Thomas to New York, 13 February to 22 February 1965.

VOYAGE 290 Eastbound and Westbound New York to Le Havre to Southampton to Bremerhaven to Southampton to Le Havre to New York, 24 February to 9 March 1965.

VOYAGE 291 Eastbound and Westbound New York to Le Havre to Southampton to Bremerhaven to Southampton to Le Havre to New York, 12 March to 25 March 1965.

VOYAGE 292 Cruise: New York to Nassau to Curaçao to St Thomas to New York, 27 March to 5 April 1965.

VOYAGE 293 Eastbound and Westbound New York to Le Havre to Southampton to Bremerhaven to Southampton to Le Havre to New York, 7 April to 20 April 1965.

VOYAGE 294 Eastbound and Westbound New York to Le Havre to Southampton to Le Havre to New York, 22 April to 3 May 1965.

VOYAGE 295 Eastbound and Westbound New York to Le Havre to Southampton to Bremerhaven to Southampton to Le Havre to New York, 5 May to 18 May 1965.

VOYAGE 296 Eastbound and Westbound New York to Le Havre to Southampton to Le Havre to New York, 20 May to 31 May 1965.

VOYAGE 297 Eastbound and Westbound New York to Le Havre to Southampton to Le Havre to New York, 2 June to 13 June 1965.

VOYAGE 298 Eastbound and Westbound New York to Le Havre to Southampton to Le Havre to New York, 14 June to 25 June 1965.

VOYAGE 299 Idle Status at Pier 86 owing to industrial strike action.

VOYAGE 300 Idle Status at Pier 86 owing to industrial strike action.

VOYAGE 301 Idle Status at Pier 86 owing to industrial strike action.

VOYAGE 302 Idle Status at Pier 86 owing to industrial strike action.

VOYAGE 303 Eastbound and Westbound New York to Le Havre to Southampton to Bremerhaven to Southampton to Le Havre to New York, 26 August to 8 September 1965.

VOYAGE 304 Eastbound and Westbound New York to Le Havre to Southampton to Le Havre to New York, 10 September to 21 September 1965.

VOYAGE 305 Eastbound and Westbound New York to Le Havre to Southampton to Bremerhaven to Southampton to Le Havre to New York, 23 September to 6 October 1965.

VOYAGE 306 Eastbound and Westbound New York to Le Havre to Southampton to Le Havre to New York, 8 October to 19 October 1965.

VOYAGE 307 Eastbound and Westbound New York to Le Havre to Southampton to Bremerhaven to Southampton to Le Havre to New York, 21 October to 3 November 1965.

VOYAGE 308 Eastbound and Westbound New York to Le Havre to Southampton to Bremerhaven to Southampton to Le Havre to New York, 6 November to 18 November 1965.
   The vessel departed from Pier 86, New York, at 16:11 on 18 November and arrived at Newport News Dry Dock at 07:16 on 19 November 1965. She departed from Newport News Dry Dock at 19:30 on 4 December and returned to Pier 86, New York, at 07:30 on 5 December 1965.

VOYAGE 309 Eastbound and Westbound New York to Le Havre to Southampton to Le Havre to New York, 9 December to 20 December 1965.

VOYAGE 310 Cruise New York to St Thomas (anchored off only) to Martinique (anchored off only) to Nassau (unscheduled) to Trinidad to Curaçao to New York 23 December 1965 to 3 January 1966.

Bad weather disrupted the calls at St Thomas and Martinique and so an extra call was made at Nassau in lieu.

VOYAGE 311 Eastbound and Westbound New York to Le Havre to Southampton to Bremerhaven to Southampton to Le Havre to New York, 5 January to 18 January 1966

VOYAGE 312 Eastbound and Westbound New York to Le Havre to Southampton to Bremerhaven to Southampton to Le Havre to New York, 20 January to 2 February 1966.

VOYAGE 313 Cruise: New York to St Thomas to Curaçao to Cristóbal to Kingston to New York 5 February to 17 February 1966.

VOYAGE 314 Eastbound and Westbound New York to Le Havre to Southampton to Bremerhaven to Southampton to Le Havre to New York, 19 February to 4 March 1966.

VOYAGE 315 Eastbound and Westbound New York to Le Havre to Southampton to Bremerhaven to Southampton to Le Havre to New York, 8 March to 21 March 1966.

VOYAGE 316 Eastbound and Westbound New York to Le Havre to Southampton to Bremerhaven to Southampton to Le Havre to New York, 24 March to 6 April 1966.

VOYAGE 317 Cruise: New York to Curaçao to St Thomas to Bermuda to New York, 8 April to 17 April 1966.

VOYAGE 318 Eastbound and Westbound New York to Le Havre to Southampton to Bremerhaven to Southampton to Le Havre to New York, 19 April to 2 May 1966.

VOYAGE 319 Eastbound and Westbound New York to Le Havre to Southampton to Bremerhaven to Southampton to Le Havre to New York, 4 May to 17 May 1966.

VOYAGE 320 Eastbound and Westbound New York to Cobh to Le Havre to Southampton to Le Havre to New York, 20 May to 31 May 1966.

Film star Joan Crawford was on the passenger list and was noted having cocktails with Captain Alexanderson. A 21in silver oar, valued at $25,000, was listed on the infantry bound for the Exhibition of Admiralty Silver Oar Maces held at National Maritime Museum at Greenwich. Dating from around 1725 and loaned by the United States District Court for the Southern District of New York, the silver oar was given a round-the-clock guard.

VOYAGE 321 Eastbound and Westbound New York to Le Havre to Southampton to Bremerhaven to Southampton to Le Havre to New York, 2 June 1966 to 15 June 1966.

VOYAGE 322 Eastbound and Westbound New York to Le Havre to Southampton to Le Havre to New York, 17 June to 28 June 1966.

VOYAGE 323 Eastbound and Westbound New York to Le Havre to Southampton to Bremerhaven to Southampton to Le Havre to New York, 30 June to 13 July 1966.

VOYAGE 324 Eastbound and Westbound New York to Le Havre to Southampton to Le Havre to New York, 15 July to 26 July 1966.

VOYAGE 325 Eastbound and Westbound New York to Le Havre to Southampton to Bremerhaven to Southampton to Le Havre to New York, 29 July to 11 August 1966.

VOYAGE 326 Eastbound and Westbound New York to Le Havre to Southampton to Le Havre to New York, 13 August to 24 August 1966.

VOYAGE 327 Eastbound and Westbound New York to Le Havre to Southampton to Le Havre to New York, 27 August to 6 September 1966.

VOYAGE 328 Eastbound and Westbound New York to Le Havre to Southampton to Bremerhaven to Southampton to Le Havre to New York, 8 September to 21 September 1966.

Hollywood film star James Stewart was on the VIP passenger list for the westbound voyage. Also on board was sixty-six-year-old Heinz Arntz, the world endurance record holder for sustained piano playing.

VOYAGE 329 Eastbound and Westbound New York to Le Havre to Southampton to Le Havre to Cobh to New York, 23 September to 4 October 1966.

VOYAGE 330 Eastbound and Westbound New York to Le Havre to Southampton to Bremerhaven to Southampton to Le Havre to New York, 7 October to 20 October 1966.

VOYAGE 331 Eastbound and Westbound New York to Le Havre to Southampton to Bremerhaven to Southampton to Le Havre to New York, 21 October to 4 November 1966.

30 October Report from David T. FitzGerald, chief purser, SS *United States*:

The United States Line Paris and Le Havre offices advised the ship to be on their guard regarding a potential troublesome passenger [Mrs X]. She had complained about her accommodation on the SS *United States* and had tied up the entire Paris office for some time. The passenger had been offered an upgrade from Tourist Class to First Class, but had refused to do so. The Paris Office instructed the ship under no circumstances to upgrade without full payment.

Soon after embarkation on the SS *United States*, Mrs X appeared at the purser's office to make her first complaint, namely that there was another passenger in her room and that there would not be enough space for all her luggage. The complaints logbook records, 'She practically forced the other passenger from the allocated room, persuading her that she should do so.'

The next complaint was that the bell in the room was not working. The ship's electrician was summoned, the bell tested and found to be in good working order.

Mrs X next summoned Morris Luft, the tourist class purser, to complain that the air-conditioning system was unsatisfactory. The ship's air-conditioning engineer attended Room C58, tested the air conditioning and found it to be in good working order.

The chief steward next received a complaint from Mrs X stating that the personnel aboard were unfriendly and some were coloured! The chief steward pointed out that he had already moved Mrs X to three different tables.

Mrs X was offered three U-Deck tourist-class rooms, of which she accepted room U-23. Despite this, Mr Austin, the chief tourist-class steward, was summoned at 04:30 hours by Mrs X with a list of further complaints.

It was agreed that the predictions of the Paris and Le Havre offices of the United States Line were correct. The passenger had created mayhem with the other passengers and staff aboard the SS *United States*. It was therefore decided that at the conclusion of Voyage 331 that this passenger would be the first to be banned from all future travel on the SS *United States*. All United States Line offices were advised of this unprecedented action.

VOYAGE 332 Eastbound and Westbound New York to Le Havre to Southampton to Bremerhaven to Southampton to Le Havre to New York, 8 November to 21 November 1966.

VOYAGE 333 Cruise: New York to Bermuda to New York, 23 November to 28 November 1966.

The ship departed from Pier 86, New York, at 18:00 on 28 November and arrived at Newport News Dry Dock at 03:24 on 29 November 1966. She departed from Newport News Dry Dock at 17:40 on 18 December and returned to Pier 86, New York, at 05:58 on 19 December 1966.

VOYAGE 334 Cruise: New York to Nassau to Cristóbal to Curaçao to St Thomas to New York, 22 December 1966 to 2 January 1967.

VOYAGE 335 Eastbound and Westbound New York to Le Havre to Southampton to Bremerhaven to Southampton to Le Havre to New York, 4 January to 17 January 1967.

VOYAGE 336 Eastbound and Westbound New York to Le Havre to Southampton to Bremerhaven to Southampton to Le Havre to New York, 20 January to 2 February 1967.

VOYAGE 337 Cruise: New York to Cristóbal to Curaçao to St Thomas to New York, 4 February to 13 February 1967.

VOYAGE 338 Eastbound and Westbound New York to Le Havre to Southampton to Bremerhaven to Southampton to Le Havre to New York 16 February to 2 March 1967.

Pages from the complaints log.

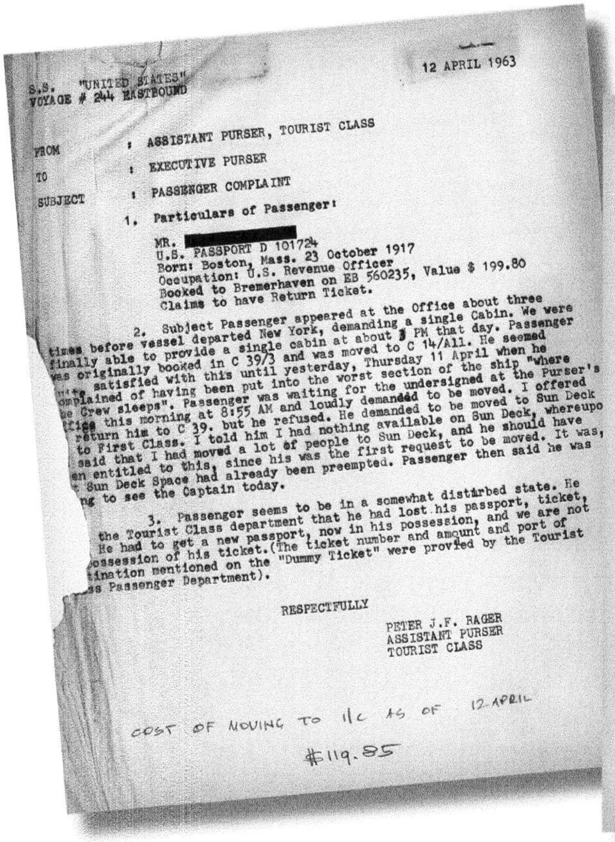

S.S. "UNITED STATES"
VOYAGE # 244 EASTBOUND

12 APRIL 1963

FROM : ASSISTANT PURSER, TOURIST CLASS
TO : EXECUTIVE PURSER
SUBJECT : PASSENGER COMPLAINT

1. Particulars of Passenger:

MR. [redacted]
U.S. PASSPORT D 101724
Born: Boston, Mass. 23 October 1917
Occupation: U.S. Revenue Officer
Booked to Bremerhaven on EB 560235, Value $ 199.80
Claims to have Return Ticket.

2. Subject Passenger appeared at the Office about three
times before vessel departed New York, demanding a single Cabin. We were
finally able to provide a single cabin at about 3 PM that day. Passenger
was originally booked in C 39/3 and was moved to C 14/All. He seemed
... satisfied with this until yesterday, Thursday 11 April when he
complained of having been put into the worst section of the ship "where
the Crew sleeps". Passenger was waiting for the undersigned at the Purser's
Office this morning at 8:55 AM and loudly demanded to be moved. I offered
return him to C 39. but he refused. He demanded to be moved to Sun Deck
to First Class. I told him I had nothing available on Sun Deck, whereupo
said that I had moved a lot of people to Sun Deck, and he should have
...en entitled to this, since his was the first request to be moved. It was,
... Sun Deck Space had already been preempted. Passenger then said he was
...ng to see the Captain today.

3. Passenger seems to be in a somewhat disturbed state. He
... the Tourist Class department that he had lost his passport, ticket,
He had to get a new passport, now in his possession, and we are not
...possession of his ticket.(The ticket number and amount and port of
...tination mentioned on the "Dummy Ticket" were provided by the Tourist
...s Passenger Department).

RESPECTFULLY

PETER J.F. RAGER
ASSISTANT PURSER
TOURIST CLASS

COST OF MOVING TO 1/C AS OF 12 APRIL
$119.85

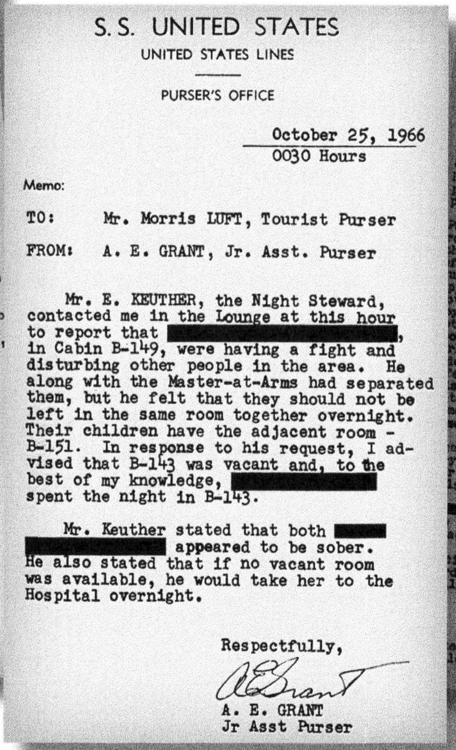

S.S. UNITED STATES
UNITED STATES LINES

PURSER'S OFFICE

October 25, 1966
0030 Hours

Memo:

TO: Mr. Morris LUFT, Tourist Purser

FROM: A. E. GRANT, Jr. Asst. Purser

Mr. E. KEUTHER, the Night Steward, contacted me in the Lounge at this hour to report that [redacted], in Cabin B-149, were having a fight and disturbing other people in the area. He along with the Master-at-Arms had separated them, but he felt that they should not be left in the same room together overnight. Their children have the adjacent room - B-151. In response to his request, I advised that B-143 was vacant and, to the best of my knowledge, [redacted] spent the night in B-143.

Mr. Keuther stated that both [redacted] appeared to be sober. He also stated that if no vacant room was available, he would take her to the Hospital overnight.

Respectfully,

A. E. Grant

A. E. GRANT
Jr Asst Purser

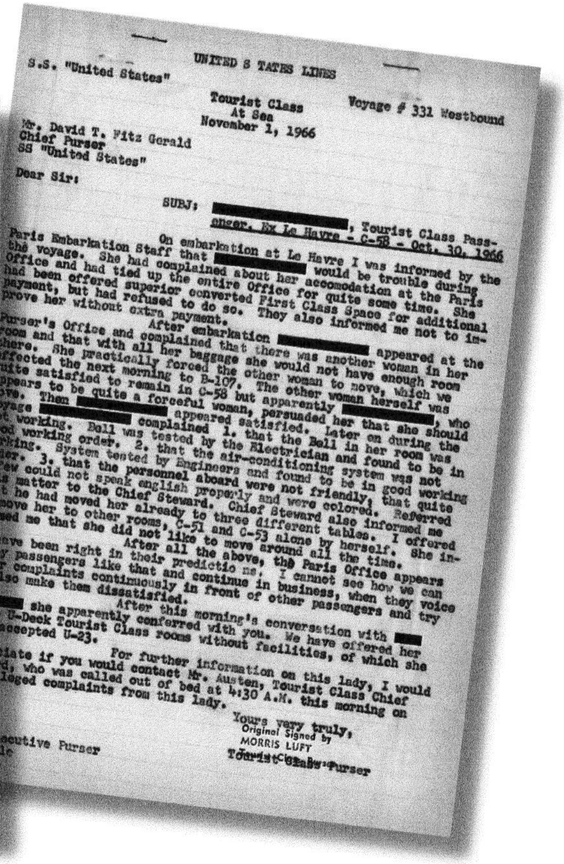

UNITED STATES LINES

S.S. "United States"

Tourist Class
At Sea
November 1, 1966

Voyage # 331 Westbound

Mr. David T. Fitz Gerald
Chief Purser
SS "United States"

Dear Sir:

SUBJ: [redacted], Tourist Class Passenger. Ex Le Havre - C-58 - Oct. 30, 1966

On embarkation at Le Havre I was informed by the
Paris Embarkation Staff that [redacted] would be trouble during
the voyage. She had complained about her accomodation at the Paris
Office and had tied up the entire Office for quite some time. She
had been offered superior converted First Class Space for additional
payment, but had refused to do so. They also informed me not to im-
prove her without extra payment.

After embarkation [redacted] appeared at the
Purser's Office and complained that there was another woman in her
room and that with all her baggage she would not have enough room
...here. She practically forced the other woman to move, which we
...ffected the next morning to B-107. The other woman herself was
...uite satisfied to remain in C-58 but apparently [redacted], who
...ppears to be quite a forceful woman, persuaded her that she should
...ove. Then [redacted] appeared satisfied. Later on during the
...oyage [redacted] complained 1. that the Bell in her room was
...t working. Bell was tested by the Electrician and found to be in
...od working order. 2. that the air-conditioning system was not
...rking. System tested by Engineers and found to be in good working
...er. 3. that the personnel aboard were not friendly, that quite
...ew could not speak english properly and were colored. Referred
...s matter to the Chief Steward. Chief Steward also informed me
...t he had moved her already to three different tables. I offered
...move her to other rooms, C-51 and C-53 alone by herself. She in-
...ed me that she did not like to move around all the time.

After all the above, the Paris Office appears
...ave been right in their predictions. I cannot see how we can
...y passengers like that and continue in business, when they voice
...r complaints continuously in front of other passengers and try
...lso make them dissatisfied.

After this morning's conversation with [redacted]
... she apparently conferred with you. We have offered her
... U-Deck Tourist Class rooms without facilities, of which she
accepted U-23.

For further information on this lady, I would
...ciate if you would contact Mr. Austen, Tourist Class Chief
...d, who was called out of bed at 4:30 A.M. this morning on
...lleged complaints from this lady.

Yours very truly,
Original Signed by
MORRIS LUFT
Tourist Class Purser

...ecutive Purser

VOYAGE 339 Cruise: New York to St Thomas to New York, 4 March to 10 March 1967.

VOYAGE 340 Cruise: New York to St Thomas to Trinidad to Curaçao to New York, 11 March to 20 March 1967.

VOYAGE 341 Eastbound and Westbound New York to Le Havre to Southampton to Bremerhaven to Southampton to Le Havre to New York, 23 March to 5 April 1967.

VOYAGE 342 Cruise: New York to Nassau to St Thomas to Martinique to Bermuda to New York, 7 April to 16 April 1967.

VOYAGE 343 Eastbound and Westbound New York to Le Havre to Southampton to Bremerhaven to Southampton to Le Havre to New York, 18 April to 1 May 1967.

VOYAGE 344 Eastbound and Westbound New York to Le Havre to Southampton to Bremerhaven to Southampton to Le Havre to New York, 3 May to 16 May 1967.

VOYAGE 345 Eastbound and Westbound New York to Cobh to Le Havre to Southampton to Le Havre to New York, 18 May to 29 May 1967.

VOYAGE 346 Eastbound and Westbound New York to Le Havre to Southampton to Bremerhaven to Southampton to Le Havre to New York, 31 May to 13 June 1967.

The Duke and Duchess of Windsor travelling aboard disembarked at Southampton to attend celebrations at London for the centenary of the birth of the late Queen Mary, at the invitation of Her Majesty the Queen. They were officially greeted at Ocean Terminal, Southampton, by HRH Lord Louis Mountbatten of Burma, who was welcomed aboard the SS *United States* by Commodore Alexanderson.

VOYAGE 347 Eastbound and Westbound New York to Le Havre to Southampton to Le Havre to New York, 15 June to 26 June 1967.

VOYAGE 348 Eastbound and Westbound New York to Le Havre to Southampton to Le Havre to New York, 29 June to 10 July 1967.

VOYAGE 349 Eastbound and Westbound New York to Le Havre to Southampton to Bremerhaven to Southampton to Le Havre to New York, 12 July to 25 July 1967.

VOYAGE 350 Eastbound and Westbound New York to Cobh to Le Havre to Southampton to Le Havre to New York, 27 July to 7 August 1967.

VOYAGE 351 Eastbound and Westbound New York to Le Havre to Southampton to Bremerhaven to Southampton to Le Havre to New York, 9 August to 22 August 1967.

VOYAGE 352 Eastbound and Westbound New York to Le Havre to Southampton to Le Havre to New York, 25 August to 5 September 1967.

VOYAGE 353 Eastbound and Westbound New York to Le Havre to Southampton to Bremerhaven to Southampton to Le Havre to New York, 7 September to 20 September 1967.

7 September The death of the designer of the SS *United States*, Mr William Francis Gibbs, was announced and the ship's ensign was flown at half-mast.

VOYAGE 354 Eastbound and Westbound New York to Le Havre to Southampton to Cherbourg to Cobh to New York, 22 September to 3 October 1967.

VOYAGE 355 Eastbound and Westbound New York to Le Havre to Southampton to Bremerhaven to Southampton to Le Havre to New York, 5 October to 18 October 1967.

VOYAGE 356 Eastbound and Westbound New York to Le Havre to Southampton to Bremerhaven to Southampton to Le Havre to New York, 20 October to 2 November 1967.
The ship departed from Pier 86, New York, at 19:09 on 2 November and arrived at Newport News Dry Dock at 07:54 on 3 November 1967. She departed from Newport News Dry Dock at 19:54 on 30 November and returned to Pier 86, New York, at 05:54 on 1 December 1967.

VOYAGE 357 Eastbound and Westbound New York to Le Havre to Southampton to Bremerhaven to Southampton to Le Havre to New York, 6 December to 19 December 1967.

VOYAGE 358 Cruise: New York to Cristóbal to Curaçao to St Thomas to Nassau to New York, 22 December 1967 to 2 January 1968.

VOYAGE 359 Eastbound and Westbound New York to Le Havre to Southampton to Bremerhaven to Southampton to Le Havre to New York, 4 January to 17 January 1968.

VOYAGE 360 Eastbound and Westbound New York to Le Havre to Southampton to Bremerhaven to Southampton to Le Havre to New York, 19 January to 1 February 1968.

VOYAGE 361 Cruise: New York to Curaçao to Rio de Janeiro to Dakar to Santa Cruz, Tenerife to Gibraltar to Lisbon to Funchal, Madeira to New York, 3 February to 2 March 1968.

VOYAGE 362 Eastbound and Westbound New York to Le Havre to Southampton to Bremerhaven to Southampton to Le Havre to New York, 6 March to 21 March 1968.

VOYAGE 363 Eastbound and Westbound New York to Le Havre to Southampton to Bremerhaven to Southampton to Le Havre to New York, 21 March to 3 April 1968.
A stowaway, David Sexton of 39 Boyden Avenue, Maplewood, New Jersey, USA, was apprehended and detained in custody to the ship's brig to await transfer to the authorities at New York.

VOYAGE 364 Cruise: New York to Cristóbal to Curaçao to St Thomas to New York, 6 April to 15 April 1968.

VOYAGE 365 Eastbound and Westbound New York to Le Havre to Southampton to Bremerhaven to Southampton to Le Havre to New York, 17 April to 30 April 1968.

VOYAGE 366 Eastbound and Westbound New York to Le Havre to Southampton to Bremerhaven to Southampton to Le Havre to New York, 2 May to 15 May 1968.

VOYAGE 367 Eastbound and Westbound New York to Cobh to Southampton to New York, 17 May to 28 May 1968.

VOYAGE 368 Eastbound and Westbound New York to Southampton to Bremerhaven to Southampton to New York, 31 May to 13 June 1968.

VOYAGE 369 Eastbound and Westbound New York to Le Havre to Southampton to Le Havre to New York, 15 June to 26 June 1968.

VOYAGE 370 Eastbound and Westbound New York to Le Havre to Southampton to Le Havre to Cobh to New York, 28 June to 9 July 1968.

VOYAGE 371 Eastbound and Westbound New York to Le Havre to Southampton to Bremerhaven to Southampton to New York, 11 July to 24 July 1968.

VOYAGE 372 New York to Cobh to Le Havre to Southampton to Le Havre to New York, 26 July to 6 August 1968.

VOYAGE 373 Eastbound and Westbound New York to Le Havre to Southampton to New York, 9 August to 20 August 1968.

VOYAGE 374 Eastbound and Westbound New York to Le Havre to Southampton to Bremerhaven to Southampton to Le Havre to New York, 22 August to 4 September 1968.

VOYAGE 375 Eastbound and Westbound New York to Le Havre to Southampton to Le Havre to Cobh to New York, 6 September to 17 September 1968.

VOYAGE 376 Eastbound and Westbound New York to Le Havre to Southampton to Bremerhaven to Southampton to Le Havre to New York, 19 September to 2 October 1968.

Sailing delayed from 12 noon until 18:45 owing to an industrial dispute.

VOYAGE 377 Eastbound and Westbound New York to Le Havre to Southampton to Bremerhaven to Southampton to Le Havre to New York, 4 October to 17 October 1968.

VOYAGE 378 Eastbound and Westbound New York to Le Havre to Southampton to Bremerhaven to Southampton to Le Havre to New York, 19 October to 1 November 1968.

VOYAGE 379 Cruise: New York to Bermuda to Lisbon to Funchal to Tenerife to Dakar to St Thomas to New York, 7 November to 25 November 1968.

The ship departed from Pier 86, New York, at 17:48 on 25 November and arrived at Newport News Dry Dock at 07:24 on 26 November 1968. She departed from Newport News Dry Dock at 23:27 on 16 December and returned to Pier 86, New York, at 10:48 on 17 December 1968.

VOYAGE 380 Cruise: New York to St Thomas to Dakar to Funchal to Tenerife to New York, 20 December 1968 to 6 January 1969.

VOYAGE 381 Logbook dated 6 January to 22 January 1969 states, 'VOYAGE 381 CANCELLED'.

VOYAGE 382 Cruise: New York to Curaçao to Rio de Janeiro to Cape Town to Port Elizabeth, South Africa to Cape Town, South Africa, to Luanda, Angola to Dakar, Senegal to Tenerife, Canary Islands to Gibraltar to Lisbon, Portugal to Funchal to New York, 23 January to 3 March 1969.

VOYAGE 383 New York to Martinique to St Thomas to New York, 5 March to 12 March 1969.

VOYAGE 384 Eastbound and Westbound New York to Le Havre to Southampton to Bremerhaven to Southampton to Le Havre to New York, 13 March to 26 March 1969.

VOYAGE 385 Cruise: New York to Funchal, Madeira to Palma, Majorca to Cannes, France to Gibraltar to Hamilton, Bermuda to New York, 28 March to 13 April 1969.

VOYAGE 386 New York to Southampton to Bremerhaven to Southampton to Le Havre to New York, 15 April to 28 April 1969.

A newspaper at sea!

VOYAGE 387 New York to Boston to Cobh to Le Havre to Southampton to Le Havre to New York, 30 April to 12 May 1969.

VOYAGE 388 Eastbound and Westbound New York to Le Havre to Southampton to Bremerhaven to Southampton to Le Havre to New York, 13 May to 26 May 1969.

VOYAGE 389 Eastbound and Westbound New York to Cherbourg to Southampton to Cherbourg to New York, 28 May to 8 June 1969.

VOYAGE 390 Eastbound and Westbound New York to Le Havre to Southampton to Bremerhaven to Southampton to Le Havre to New York, 10 June to 23 June 1969.

VOYAGE 391 Eastbound and Westbound New York to Le Havre to Southampton to Le Havre to New York, 24 June to 6 July 1969.

VOYAGE 392 Eastbound and Westbound New York to Le Havre to Southampton to Le Havre to New York, 7 July to 18 July 1969.

VOYAGE 393 Eastbound and Westbound New York to Le Havre to Southampton to Bremerhaven to Southampton to Le Havre to New York, 19 July to 1 August 1969.

VOYAGE 394 Eastbound and Westbound New York to Le Havre to Southampton to Le Havre to New York, 3 August to 14 August 1969.

VOYAGE 395 Eastbound and Westbound New York to Le Havre to Southampton to Le Havre to New York, 15 August to 26 August 1969.

VOYAGE 396 Eastbound and Westbound New York to Le Havre to Southampton to Bremerhaven to Southampton to Le Havre to New York, 28 August to 10 September 1969.

VOYAGE 397 Eastbound and Westbound New York to Le Havre to Southampton to Le Havre to New York, 12 September to 23 September 1969.

VOYAGE 398 Eastbound and Westbound New York to Le Havre to Southampton to Bremerhaven to Southampton to Cherbourg to New York, 26 September to 9 October 1969.

VOYAGE 399 Eastbound and Westbound New York to Le Havre to Southampton to Bremerhaven to Southampton to Le Havre to New York, 10 October to 21 October 1969.

VOYAGE 400 Eastbound and Westbound New York to Le Havre to Southampton to Bremerhaven to Southampton to Le Havre to New York, 25 October to 7 November 1969.

VOYAGE 3 259

This is a description of a departure from New York on board the SS *United States* using for reference the deck logbook, official engineering logbook and telegraph book covering this voyage.

At midnight on a cold wet Wednesday, 6 November 1963, two enormous illuminated red funnels, the gigantic black hull with sparkling silver pinholes radiating light from hidden port holes and the glistening white superstructure rising high above Pier 86 at West 46th Street, New York, proclaimed that the SS *United States* was in port. She lay silent with not a wisp of smoke emanating from those funnels. High above on the upper deck patrolled a lonely nightwatchman, Lookout Carson, gazing across the Hudson. The dark silence was broken only by a whistling workman trailing up and down the gangplanks with his tools. On the bridge, Mr A. Moreno made the first entry into the deck log book for Voyage 259:

00:00 to 04:00: Routine inspections and reports. Strict fire and security watch maintained. Lights, lines and gangways tended. Weather: Overcast, light rain.

At 08:00 enthusiastic painters set to work with their paint brushes, touching up the vast 990ft-long black hull of the superliner, perched precariously on flimsy wooden planks secured by an array of overhanging ropes. By now four gangs of longshoremen were aboard to resume discharging from Hatch 5 and loading Hatches 1, 3 and 4, beginning with huge gas-guzzling American limos which were carefully lowered into the hold.

Work continued uninterrupted, preparing the SS *United States* for the voyage sailing at 12 noon the next day. Then, suddenly and unannounced, at 08:30 on Thursday 7 November, the deafening fire alarm sounded, echoing around Pier 86.

08:30: Sounded alarm for fire drill. All hands mustered at fire stations.
08:32: Emergency squad mustered and dispatched to scene of emergency with full equipment.
08:33: 5 hoses led out Fwd and Aft. Full pressure applied.
08:50: Secured from drills.
09:00: Commenced embarkation of passengers.

'There she is, Mister," shouted the yellow cab taxi driver in his distinctive New York accent, pointing to two enormous red funnels peering above the Pier 86 terminal building of the United States Line. Flags fluttered from the masts on the pier and taxis crowded outside the busy main entrance with its red, white and blue awning. A sign proudly proclaimed, 'United States Line *United States* sailing noon today.'

Luggage, if not delivered ahead, was now entrusted to the porters with their special loading planks. Passengers were stopped inside the pier for ticket processing while visitors made a contribution to the local seamen's fund in return for a boarding pass. Excited passengers boarding the SS *United States* now made their way to the distinctive class areas: first class then cabin and tourist class. Visitors did the same. All around the main hall there was noise and excitement as hundreds of *bon voyage* baskets were loaded aboard. As passengers and visitors made their way aboard the Big U, a band began to serenade playing *In the good old*

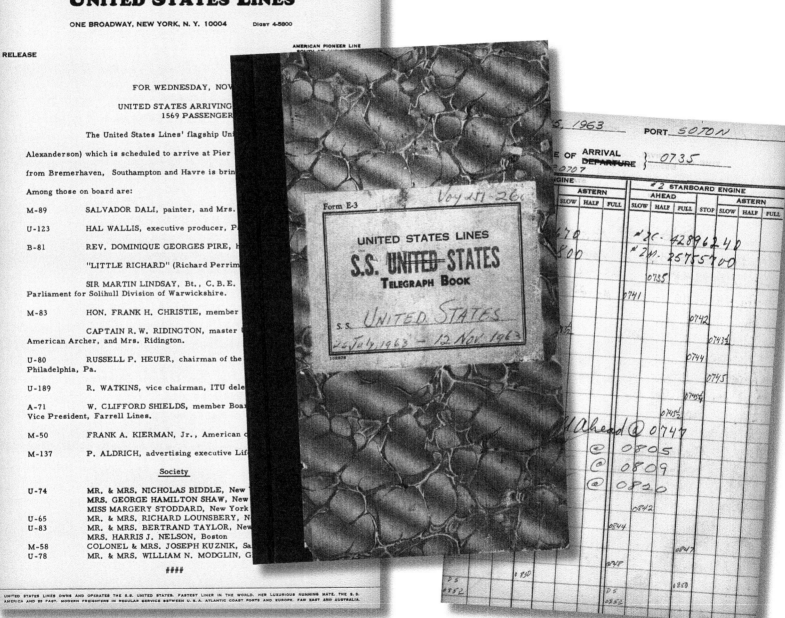

Press release and telegraph
log book.

summer time, adding to the thrill of the occasion. As soon as passengers stepped aboard, a smartly uniformed steward came forward to escort them to their stateroom.

Meanwhile, Esso barges drew alongside, filling up the thirsty oil bunkers. A steady stream of trucks entered and left Pier 86, crammed full of supplies for the voyage. These included:

Dry stores:	58,680lb
Dairy	61,025lb
Fish (shell, fresh, smoke and pickled)	13,048lb
Fresh vegetables	32,140lb
Frozen juices	15,903lb
Fresh juice	37,098lb
Meat	59,512lb
Poultry	14,150lb
Potatoes	17,000lb
Ice cubes	1 ton
Ice cream	3 tons
Cigarettes and tobacco	1 ton
Wine and liquor	4 tons
Beer	15 tons
Work deck stores	11 tons
Linen	35 tons
Miscellaneous	4 tons

The deck logbook records:

10:00: Tested and examined whistles, telegraphs, steering gear, navigation lights, general alarm, radars and communications systems. All in apparent good order. Synchronized bridge and engine room clocks.

The time leading up to 11:30 just appeared to slip away as excited passengers and visitors explored the ship, peering into the ballroom, testing the chairs in the dining room, inspecting the decks and equipment and snapping photographs of as much as possible. At 11:33 the liner's Tyfon whistles sounded a single blast and there followed an announcement on the Tannoy loudspeaker system that all visitors must leave the ship.

11:30: Deck logbook, engine room telegraph log and official engineering logbook all record:

Stand by engines.

At 11:40 the Moran tug, *Alice Moran*, arrived on station assisting forward, and Docking Pilot W. Snyder and Sandy Hook Pilot J. Sullivan arrived on the bridge to assist the Master. Ten minutes later the search for stowaways, narcotics and contraband was completed. In overcast and heavy rain, the Moran tug, *Christine Moran*, made fast on the starboard stern chock and the hawsers were released in readiness to depart. Almost with military precision the gangways were unhooked and excited passengers surged towards the deck rails to watch them disappear into the dark caverns of Pier 86.

12:00: Three blasts from the Tyfon whistles, two short and one long, announced to New York that the SS *United States* had sailed. A cloud of ink black smoke rose from the two funnels and slowly, very slowly, the great liner reluctantly backed out into the Hudson, fighting against the currents. The movement astern was so slow that many of the cheering passengers and their waving families and friends on the pier did not realise immediately that the SS *United States* was underway. It took a full nine minutes before she was all clear of the dock and the starboard swing could commence. The Moran tug *Christine* began pushing hard on the SS *United States* starboard quarter while *Alice* pressed hard against the starboard bow in order to pivot the enormous liner, stern first, up river to face her towards the sea. This was successfully achieved by 12:17 and the Docking Pilot Snyder handed over command to Sandy Hook Pilot Sullivan. Pilot Snyder then made his way down to the Port shell door and transferred at 12:24 via a precarious Jacob's ladder to an accompanying Moran tug ready for his next job. Meanwhile the SS *United States* cautiously made her way down the Hudson watched by curious spectators from Battery Park. By 13:10 the sleek liner had passed under the Narrows Bridge. With his job completed, Pilot Sullivan now also safely departed via the shell door to a waiting launch at 14:06. Only now could the speed be increased, at first to 100rpm then to 140rpm taking her up to 30 knots. Like a bird set free from a cage the SS *United States* was out in the Atlantic pitching moderately in 'a very rough and heavy confused swell.'

PHOTOGRAPHIC

4

RECORD

UNITED STATES LINES
CABIN CLASS
STATEROOM

UNITED STATES LINES
CABIN CLASS
BAGGAGE ROOM

UNITED STATES LINES
O
CABIN CLASS

UNITED STATES LINES
I
FIRST CLASS

UNITED STATES LINES
U
TOURIST CLASS

United States Lines

UNITED STATES LINES
CABIN CLASS
HOLD

A selection of ephemera from the SS *United States*.

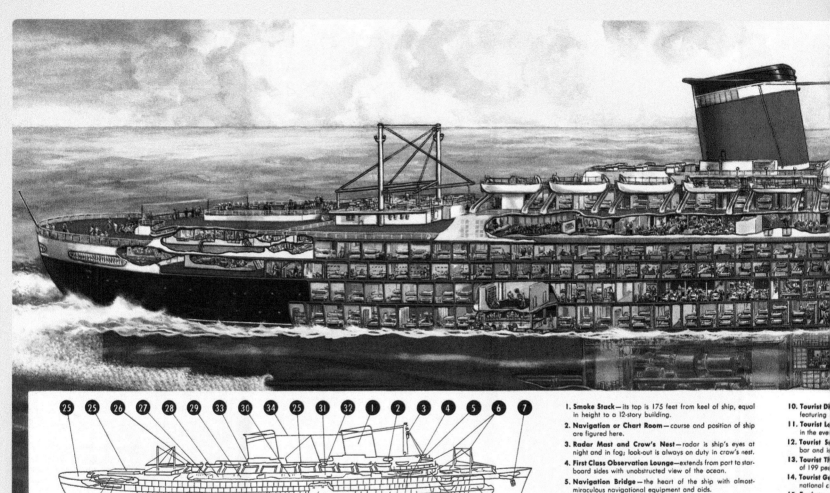

1. **Smoke Stack**—its top is 175 feet from keel of ship, equal in height to a 12-story building.
2. **Navigation or Chart Room**—course and position of ship are figured here.
3. **Radar Mast and Crow's Nest**—radar is ship's eyes at night and in fog; look-out is always on duty in crow's nest.
4. **First Class Observation Lounge**—extends from port to starboard sides with unobstructed view of the ocean.
5. **Navigation Bridge**—the heart of the ship with almost-miraculous navigational equipment and aids.
6. **Kingposts**—with boom is used to raise or lower cargo.
7. **Anchor & Cable Chain**—latest in naval design and electrically operated.
8. **Garage**—space for cars which need no special preparation for voyage.
9. **Hospital**—modern with fully equipped operating room.

10. **Tourist Di**
featuring
11. **Tourist Le**
in the eve
12. **Tourist S**
bar and is
13. **Tourist Th**
of 199 pe
14. **Tourist Ge**
national c
15. **Engines**—
this lower
16. **Store Roo**
of troops
17. **First Clas**
the finest

Cutaway view of the SS *United States*.

POSITION OF OBSERVER—420+ FEET FROM CENTER OF SHIP AT HORIZON HEIGHT

46 people; has modern decor
tical motifs.

and writing rooms; dancing

nds full width of ship; has
ed for relaxation.

able with a seating capacity

inute kitchen, providing inter-

eed turbines are located in

ugh to care for a full division
s non-stop.

ecorated in red and white;
ental dishes are served here.

18. **Galley**—ultra modern kitchens feature radar stoves.
19. **Cabin Class Dining Room**—a charming setting for gracious dining at sea.
20. **Shafts & Propellers**—powerful shafts transmit power from turbines to the giant propellers.
21. **Gymnasium**—every latest type of gymnastic equipment.
22. **Swimming Pool**—made of monel metal, it is surrounded by beach and lounge area.
23. **Cabin Class Lounge**—decorated with modern motif; has a 17 x 26 foot dance floor for dancing in the evening.
24. **Cabin Class Smoking Room**—its three sides face on the enclosed promenade deck.
25. **Play Decks**—open to the sun for lounging or playing of all types of deck sports.
26. **Life Boats**—one of 22 aluminum life boats, non-sinkable and fully fire proof, which can accommodate 3000 persons.

27. **First Class and Cabin Class Theatre**—seating 352 persons, it is fitted with modern acoustics; shows first-run films.
28. **Shopping Center**—offers wide variety of merchandise to suit every taste and purse.
29. **First Class Smoking Room**—large lounge room featuring huge aluminum maps of the world.
30. **Navajo Cocktail Lounge**—an intimate room decorated with Navajo sand paintings.
31. **First Class Ballroom**—center of social life; afternoon teas and dancing at night to Meyer Davis orchestra.
32. **Kennels**—clean modern kennels for pets; veterinarian in constant attendance.
33. **Play Room**—three play rooms aboard ship provide a liliputian playland for the younger set.
34. **Aerials**—these stretch between the largest smoke stacks of any ship in the world.

Staterooms: There are 694 staterooms, located on eight of the Superliner's 12 decks. Each of these staterooms is equipped with a telephone from which calls may be made to any other part of the ship or to any telephone ashore.

Elevators: There are 18 elevators in all parts of the ship for the convenience of passengers.

General Dimensions: The Superliner UNITED STATES is 990 feet long, 101.5 feet wide, with a gross tonnage of 53,330.

The S.S. UNITED STATES was designed by Gibbs & Cox, Inc. and built by the Newport News (Va.) Shipbuilding and Dry Dock Company.

Assorted ephemera from the SS *United States*.

1969 PASSENGER FARES

UNITED STATES LINES

1969

Passenger Fares

S.S. UNITED STATES

World's Fastest Ship

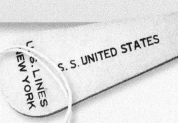

S.S. UNITED STATES

U.S. LINES
NEW YORK

UNITED STATES LINES

TOURIST CLASS
STATEROOM

S.S. UNITED
STATES

UNITED STATES LINES

TOURIST CLASS
HOLD

Cruising in the Caribbean sunshine is conducive to fun and frolic and frequently gives rise to colorful and sometimes dazzling masquerade parties. These cruise travelers are obviously enjoying themselves.

A cooling or stimulating drink at one of the United States' ten bars along with some sparkling conversation is a relaxing and enjoyable pastime either on a North Atlantic trip or on cruise. Come on aboard and enjoy both.

Shuffleboard requires just the right [...] for relax[...]

Attractive, roomy Cabin Class stateroom with two full-size single beds and a disappearing "Pullman."

The ship's two large theatres attract many who like first-run movies, with selected short subjects and many "who-done-its" for afternoon, small-fry entertainment.

Fine food, plentifully and elegantly-served is traditional on the s.s. United States. Delectable, eye-taking cruise buffets are added features of the Caribbean runs.

Come on in—the water's fine says the signal-flag legend on the ship's swimming pool. And a lot of relaxing passengers do just that.

The youngsters are never forgotten on a United States' trip—Atlantic or Caribbean. In addition to playrooms, with attendants in all classes, First, Cabin and Tourist, there are special ball-room parties set to good music.

Bon Voyage is the chant from the pier for happy young passengers as the United States sails amid a swirling storm of paper streamers.

Passengers enjoy a pre-dinner cocktail in one of the many suites aboard the s.s. United States.

Flowers help to set off the huge, first-class stateroom with its traditional port-[...] out on the blue-green Atlantic or Caribbean.

When you sail aboard the superb s.s. United States, you take a maiden voyage—an ocean trip of the future. For the big 52,000-ton superliner, while mature enough to have made an everlasting impression of ease, of pleasure, of beauty, on scores of thousands of former passengers, is still years ahead of her time.

The marvel of her engineering features built into a sleek 990-foot hull are further advanced than many liners still on the ways or drawing boards. They made it possible for her to break the North Atlantic speed record with ridiculous ease. They made her the safest ship on any ocean.

Her twenty-six public rooms are exquisite blends of the finest artwork, luxurious furnishings, appealing architectural design and color and, appointments to match every mood—gaiety, comfort and relaxation; social mingling, conviviality, pastime gaming, among others.

Her 672 First, Cabin and Tourist-class staterooms, all fully airconditioned, with individual climate control, are extraordinarily large. They have extra closet space, downy beds for 1,700 travelers, comfortable chairs, full-length mirrors, dressing tables and other furnishings. Her colors, fabrics, fittings are a symphony in decor.

Recreation, exercise in the salt-tanged atmosphere that pervades her miles of promenade decks, her numerous open sports decks are rejuvenating, healthful attributes of this fine ship. For those inclined to more strenuous activities there are the modern, well equipped gymnasium, the large indoor swimming pool. And for those who prefer merely to relax, there are the quiet nooks with their blanketed deck chairs outdoors or within the glass-enclosed promenade, for thoughtful reflection of a best seller's message, or perhaps for a nap, or maybe even just for detached, pleasant and unworried consideration of a friendly co-traveler's viewpoints on this planet and its raison d'etre.

Not to be forgotten is the excellent cuisine, which features the outstanding delectables of five continents, and which takes on added gourmet appeal because of the courteous and instant service that is synonymous with the name, s.s. United States.

Another feature aboard the liner is the night life. There's dancing to the lilting, romantic strains of Meyer Davis orchestras, professional entertainment, the fun of participating in the ship's mileage pool, the bingo games, bridge tournaments, the theatres with their first-run films, the enjoyment of a friendly drink with engaging co-passengers.

All these and many more interesting prospects are at your command on a salubrious voyage aboard the Superliner United States on her traditional North Atlantic Ocean runs to Havre, Southampton and to Bremerhaven. All these with a fascinating, tropical tinge are yours, too, on one of the exotic West Indies cruises the big American-flag liner makes each year.

See your Travel Agent for further details. Or telephone United States Lines, One Broadway, New York, New York—Digby 4-5800.

▲ The large, main dining room of the United States is a perfect setting for perfect food. Its attractive decor, snowy linens, fine silver and absolute cleanliness add to the enjoyment of meals superbly served by courteous waiters.

▼ Meyer Davis, whose name is a tradition in the music world, provides the orchestras aboard the United States for dancing and for the dinner music . . . the fine touch that makes every evening's gourmet meal of your crossing an event.

SAFETY INFORMATION
The S.S. United States registered in the United States of America meets International Safety Standards for new ships developed in 1960. The vessel meets the 1966 Fire Safety Requirements.

SPECIAL NOTICE TO PASSENGERS

For your protection during the time the vessel is at the pier we urge you to keep your valuables with you, or securely <u>locked</u> in your cabin, should you go on deck prior to the departure.

We will appreciate your cooperation to avoid possible losses of personal property during the hours visitors are on board.

Valuables should be checked at the Purser's Office after sailing for safekeeping during the voyage.

UNITED STATES LINES

60977

LIFE BOAT DRILL

Today at 4:00 p.m. on Sun-deck.
International law requires every ship to hold a Boat Drill as soon as possible after sailing time. All passengers will kindly attend the drill wearing their life belts.
See directions posted in your cabin.

RESTAURANT:
Breakfast . . . . 8:00 A. M.
Luncheon . . . . 12:15 P. M.
Dinner . . . . 6:45 P. M.
DOORS CLOSE AT 9:15 P. M.
TABLE No. . . . .
Passengers are earnestly requested to be at meals at designated times.
The Management

EARLY SITTING   Tourist Class
Breakfast . . . . 8:00 A. M.
Luncheon . . . . 12:15 P. M.
Dinner . . . . 6:00 P. M.
T   TABLE No. . . . .
Passengers are earnestly requested to be at meals at designated times.
The Management

FORM P-52

S. S. UNITED STATES **URGENT**

Room _____

IN ORDER TO FACILITATE DEBARKATION AT NEW YORK, PLEASE PRESENT YOUR TRAVEL DOCUMENTS AT THE PURSER'S OFFICE TOGETHER WITH THE ATTACHED FORM.

PRINTED IN U.S.A. 4-66
62425

S.S. UNITED STATES
WORLD'S FASTEST SHIP

United States Lines

SOUVENIR LOG

Passenger notices, timetables and daily programmes.

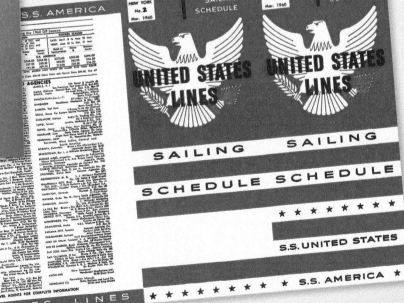

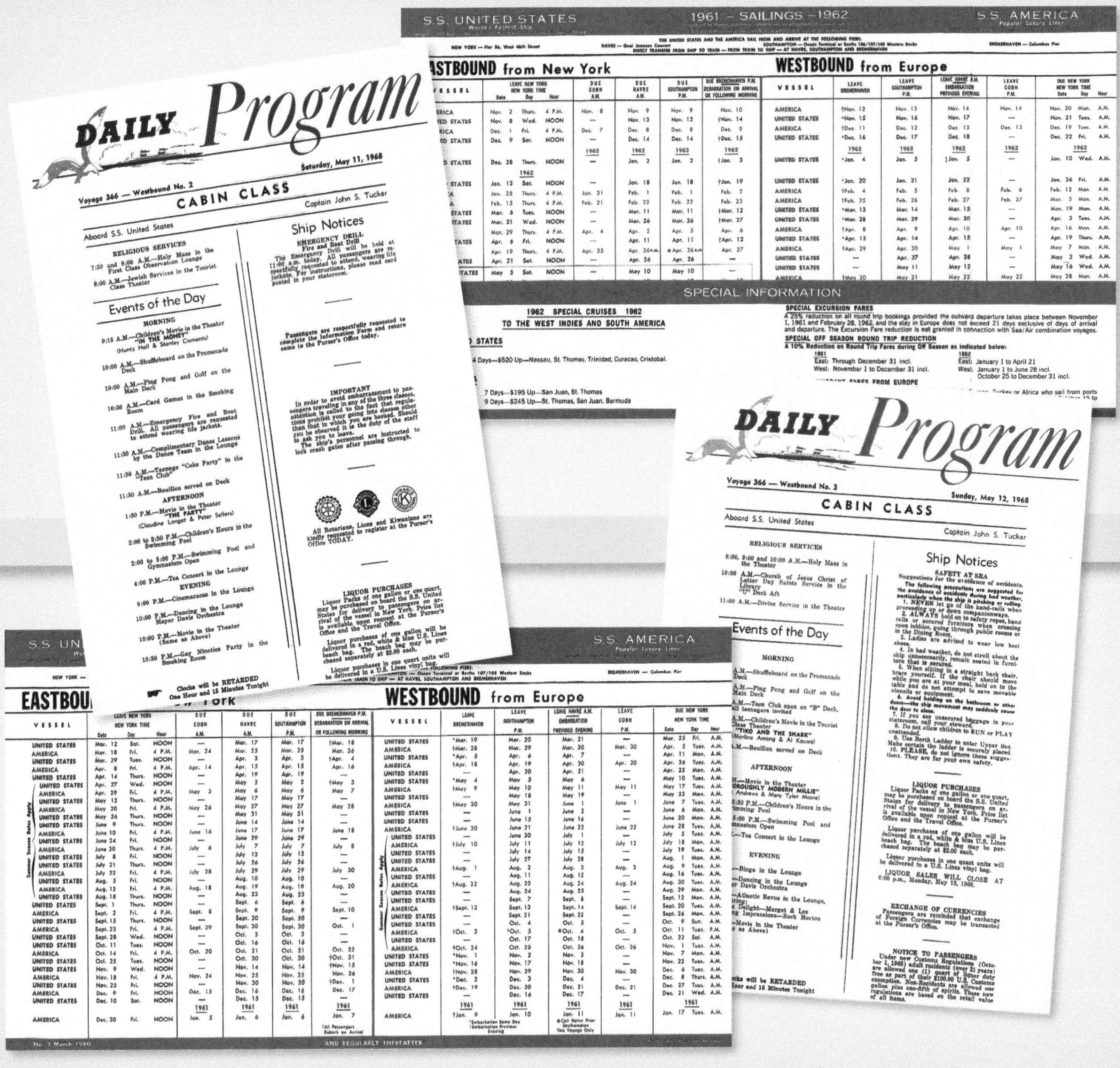

DAILY *Program*

Saturday, May 11, 1968

Voyage 366 — Westbound No. 2

CABIN CLASS

Aboard S.S. United States

Captain John S. Tucker

RELIGIOUS SERVICES

7:30 and 8:00 A.M.—Holy Mass in the First Class Observation Lounge

8:00 A.M.—Jewish Services in the Tourist Class Theater

Events of the Day

MORNING

9:15 A.M.—Children's Movie in the Theater "IN THE MONEY" (Huntz Hall & Stanley Clements)

10:00 A.M.—Shuffleboard on the Promenade Deck

10:00 A.M.—Ping Pong and Golf on the Main Deck

10:30 A.M.—Card Games in the Smoking Room

11:00 A.M.—Emergency Fire and Boat Drill. All passengers are requested to attend wearing life jackets.

11:30 A.M.—Complimentary Dance Lessons by the Dance Team in the Lounge

11:30 A.M.—Teenage "Coke Party" in the "Teen Club"

11:30 A.M.—Bouillon served on Deck

AFTERNOON

1:30 P.M.—Movie in the Theater "THE PARTY" (Claudine Longet & Peter Sellers)

2:00 to 3:30 P.M.—Children's Hours in the Swimming Pool

2:00 to 5:00 P.M.—Swimming Pool and Gymnasium Open

4:00 P.M.—Tea Concert in the Lounge

EVENING

9:00 P.M.—Cinemaraces in the Lounge

10:00 P.M.—Dancing in the Lounge Meyer Davis Orchestra

10:00 P.M.—Movie in the Theater (Same as Above)

10:30 P.M.—Gay Nineties Party in the Smoking Room

Clocks will be RETARDED One Hour and 15 Minutes Tonight

Ship Notices

EMERGENCY DRILL
Fire and Boat Drill

The Emergency Drill will be held at 11:00 a.m. today. All passengers are respectfully requested to attend, wearing life jackets. For instructions, please read card posted in your stateroom.

Passengers are respectfully requested to complete the Information Form and return same to the Purser's Office today.

IMPORTANT

In order to avoid embarrassment to passengers traveling in any of the three classes, attention is called to the fact that regulations prohibit your going into classes other than that in which you are booked. Should you be observed it is the duty of the staff to ask you to leave.

The ship's personnel are instructed to lock crash gates after passing through.

All Rotarians, Lions and Kiwanians are kindly requested to register at the Purser's Office TODAY.

LIQUOR PURCHASES

Liquor Packs of one gallon or one quart, may be purchased on board the S.S. United States for delivery to passengers on arrival of the vessel in New York. Price list is available upon request at the Purser's Office and the Travel Office.

Liquor purchases of one gallon will be delivered in a red, white & blue U.S. Lines beach bag. The beach bag may be purchased separately at $2.00 each.

Liquor purchases in one quart units will be delivered in a U.S. Lines vinyl bag.

S.S. UNITED STATES — World's Fastest Ship

1961 — SAILINGS — 1962

S.S. AMERICA — Popular Luxury Liner

THE UNITED STATES AND THE AMERICA SAIL FROM AND ARRIVE AT THE FOLLOWING PIERS:

NEW YORK — Pier 86, West 46th Street — HAVRE — Quai Joannes Couvert — SOUTHAMPTON — Ocean Terminal or Berths 106/107/108 Western Docks — BREMERHAVEN — Columbus Pier

DIRECT TRANSFER FROM SHIP TO TRAIN — FROM TRAIN TO SHIP — AT HAVRE, SOUTHAMPTON AND BREMERHAVEN

EASTBOUND from New York

VESSEL	Leave New York, New York Time: Date	Day	Hour	Due Cobh A.M.	Due Havre A.M.	Due Southampton P.M.	Due Bremerhaven P.M. Debarkation on Arrival or Following Morning
...ERICA	Nov. 2	Thurs.	4 P.M.	Nov. 8	Nov. 9	Nov. 9	Nov. 10
...TED STATES	Nov. 8	Wed.	NOON	—	Nov. 13	Nov. 13	†Nov. 14
...RICA	Dec. 1	Fri.	4 P.M.	Dec. 7	Dec. 8	Dec. 8	Dec. 9
...ED STATES	Dec. 9	Sat.	NOON	—	Dec. 14	Dec. 14	†Dec. 15
				1962	1962	1962	1962
...D STATES	Dec. 28	Thurs.	NOON	—	Jan. 2	Jan. 2	†Jan. 3
	1962						
...STATES	Jan. 13	Sat.	NOON	—	Jan. 18	Jan. 18	†Jan. 19
...A	Jan. 25	Thurs.	4 P.M.	Jan. 31	Feb. 1	Feb. 1	Feb. 2
...A	Feb. 15	Thurs.	4 P.M.	Feb. 21	Feb. 22	Feb. 22	Feb. 23
...STATES	Mar. 6	Tues.	NOON	—	Mar. 11	Mar. 11	†Mar. 12
...STATES	Mar. 21	Wed.	NOON	—	Mar. 26	Mar. 26	†Mar. 27
	Mar. 29	Thurs.	4 P.M.	Apr. 4	Apr. 5	Apr. 5	Apr. 6
...TATES	Apr. 6	Fri.	NOON	—	Apr. 11	Apr. 11	†Apr. 12
	Apr. 19	Thurs.	4 P.M.	Apr. 25	Apr. 26 P.M.	●Apr. 26 A.M.	Apr. 27
...STATES	Apr. 21	Sat.	NOON	—	Apr. 26	Apr. 26	—
...STATES	May 5	Sat.	NOON	—	May 10	May 10	—

WESTBOUND from Europe

VESSEL	Leave Bremerhaven	Leave Southampton P.M.	Leave Havre A.M. Embarkation Previous Evening	Leave Cobh P.M.	Due New York, New York Time: Date	Day	Hour
AMERICA	†Nov. 12	Nov. 13	Nov. 14	Nov. 14	Nov. 20	Mon.	A.M.
UNITED STATES	*Nov. 15	Nov. 16	Nov. 17	—	Nov. 21	Tues.	A.M.
AMERICA	†Dec. 11	Dec. 12	Dec. 13	Dec. 13	Dec. 19	Tues.	A.M.
UNITED STATES	*Dec. 16	Dec. 17	Dec. 18	—	Dec. 22	Fri.	A.M.
	1962	1962	1962	1962	1962		
UNITED STATES	*Jan. 4	Jan. 5	†Jan. 5	—	Jan. 10	Wed.	A.M.
UNITED STATES	*Jan. 20	Jan. 21	Jan. 22	—	Jan. 26	Fri.	A.M.
AMERICA	†Feb. 4	Feb. 5	Feb. 6	Feb. 6	Feb. 12	Mon.	A.M.
AMERICA	†Feb. 25	Feb. 26	Feb. 27	Feb. 27	Mar. 5	Mon.	A.M.
UNITED STATES	*Mar. 13	Mar. 14	Mar. 15	—	Mar. 19	Mon.	A.M.
UNITED STATES	*Mar. 28	Mar. 29	Mar. 30	—	Apr. 3	Tues.	A.M.
AMERICA	†Apr. 8	Apr. 9	Apr. 10	Apr. 10	Apr. 16	Mon.	A.M.
UNITED STATES	*Apr. 13	Apr. 14	Apr. 15	—	Apr. 19	Thurs.	A.M.
AMERICA	†Apr. 29	Apr. 30	May 1	May 1	May 7	Mon.	A.M.
UNITED STATES	—	Apr. 27	Apr. 28	—	May 2	Wed.	A.M.
UNITED STATES	—	May 11	May 12	—	May 16	Wed.	A.M.
AMERICA	†May 20	May 21	May 22	May 22	May 28	Mon.	A.M.

SPECIAL INFORMATION

1962 SPECIAL CRUISES 1962
TO THE WEST INDIES AND SOUTH AMERICA

...D STATES

...4 Days—$520 Up—Nassau, St. Thomas, Trinidad, Curacao, Cristobal.

7 Days—$195 Up—San Juan, St. Thomas

9 Days—$245 Up—St. Thomas, San Juan, Bermuda

SPECIAL EXCURSION FARES

A 25% reduction on all round trip bookings provided the outward departure takes place between November 1, 1961 and February 28, 1962, and the stay in Europe does not exceed 21 days exclusive of days of arrival and departure. The Excursion Fare reduction is not granted in connection with Sea/Air combination voyages.

SPECIAL OFF SEASON ROUND TRIP REDUCTION

A 10% Reduction on Round Trip Fares during Off Season as indicated below:

1961
East: Through December 31 incl.
West: November 1 to December 31 incl.

1962
East: January 1 to April 21
West: January 1 to June 28 incl.
October 25 to December 31 incl.

...FARES FROM EUROPE

...Turkey or Africa who sail from ports ... October 15 to

DAILY *Program*

Voyage 366 — Westbound No. 3

Sunday, May 12, 1968

CABIN CLASS

Aboard S.S. United States

Captain John S. Tucker

RELIGIOUS SERVICES

8:00, 9:00 and 10:00 A.M.—Holy Mass in the Theater

10:00 A.M.—Church of Jesus Christ of Latter Day Saints Service in the Library "U" Deck Aft

11:00 A.M.—Divine Service in the Theater

Events of the Day

MORNING

...A.M.—Shuffleboard on the Promenade Deck

...A.M.—Ping Pong and Golf on the Main Deck

...A.M.—Teen Club open on "B" Deck, all teenagers invited

...A.M.—Children's Movie in the Tourist Class Theater "TIKO AND THE SHARK" (Marline Among & Al Kauwe)

...A.M.—Bouillon served on Deck

AFTERNOON

...M.—Movie in the Theater ...OROUGHLY MODERN MILLIE" (...Andrews & Mary Tyler Moore)

...3:30 P.M.—Children's Hours in the ...imming Pool

...5:00 P.M.—Swimming Pool and ...mnasium Open

...—Tea Concert in the Lounge

EVENING

...—Bingo in the Lounge

...—Dancing in the Lounge ...er Davis Orchestra

...—Atlantic Revue in the Lounge, ...ring: ...e Delight—Marget & Lee ...ng Impressions—Rock Morton

...—Movie in the Theater (...e as Above)

...ocks will be RETARDED ...Hour and 15 Minutes Tonight

Ship Notices

SAFETY AT SEA

Suggestions for the avoidance of accidents.

The following precautions are suggested for the avoidance of accidents during bad weather, particularly when the ship is pitching or rolling.

1. NEVER let go of the hand-rails when proceeding up or down companionways.
2. ALWAYS hold on to safety ropes, hand rails or secured furniture when crossing open lobbies, going through public rooms or in the Dining Room.
3. Ladies are advised to wear low heel shoes.
4. In bad weather, do not stroll about the ship unnecessarily, remain seated in furniture that is secured.
5. When sitting in a straight back chair, brace yourself. If the chair should move while you are at your meal, hold on to the table and do not attempt to save movable utensils or equipment.
6. **Avoid holding on the bathroom or other doors—the ship movement may suddenly cause the door to close.**
7. If you see unsecured baggage in your stateroom, call your steward.
8. Do not allow children to RUN or PLAY unattended.
9. Use Berth Ladder to enter Upper Bed. Make certain the ladder is securely placed.
10. PLEASE, do not ignore these suggestions. They are for your own safety.

LIQUOR PURCHASES

Liquor Packs of one gallon or one quart, may be purchased on board the S.S. United States for delivery to passengers on arrival of the vessel in New York. Price list is available upon request at the Purser's Office and the Travel Office.

Liquor purchases of one gallon will be delivered in a red, white & blue U.S. Lines beach bag. The beach bag may be purchased separately at $2.00 each.

Liquor purchases in one quart units will be delivered in a U.S. Lines vinyl bag.

LIQUOR SALES WILL CLOSE AT 6:00 p.m., Monday, May 13, 1968.

EXCHANGE OF CURRENCIES

Passengers are reminded that exchange of Foreign Currencies may be transacted at the Purser's Office.

NOTICE TO PASSENGERS

Under new Customs Regulations (October 1, 1965) adult residents (over 21 years) are allowed one (1) quart of liquor duty free as part of their $100.00 U.S. Customs exemption. Non-Residents are allowed one gallon plus one-fifth of spirits. These new regulations are based on the retail value of all items.

S.S. UN...

S.S. AMERICA — Popular Luxury Liner

NEW YORK — ... SOUTHAMPTON — Ocean Terminal or Berths 107/108 Western Docks — BREMERHAVEN — Columbus Pier

...TRAIN TO SHIP — AT HAVRE, SOUTHAMPTON AND BREMERHAVEN

EASTBOU... ...York

VESSEL	Leave New York, New York Time: Date	Day	Hour	Due Cobh A.M.	Due Havre A.M.	Due Southampton P.M.	Due Bremerhaven P.M. Debarkation on Arrival or Following Morning
UNITED STATES	Mar. 12	Sat.	NOON	—	Mar. 17	Mar. 17	†Mar. 18
AMERICA	Mar. 18	Fri.	4 P.M.	Mar. 24	Mar. 25	Mar. 25	Mar. 26
UNITED STATES	Mar. 29	Tues.	NOON	—	Apr. 3	Apr. 3	†Apr. 4
AMERICA	Apr. 8	Fri.	4 P.M.	Apr. 14	Apr. 15	Apr. 15	Apr. 16
UNITED STATES	Apr. 14	Thurs.	NOON	—	Apr. 19	Apr. 19	—
UNITED STATES	Apr. 27	Wed.	NOON	—	May 2	May 2	†May 3
AMERICA	Apr. 29	Fri.	4 P.M.	May 5	May 6	May 6	May 7
UNITED STATES	May 12	Thurs.	NOON	—	May 17	May 17	—
AMERICA	May 20	Fri.	4 P.M.	May 26	May 27	May 27	May 28
UNITED STATES	May 26	Thurs.	NOON	—	May 31	May 31	—
UNITED STATES	June 9	Thurs.	NOON	—	June 14	June 14	—
AMERICA	June 10	Fri.	4 P.M.	June 16	June 17	June 17	June 18
UNITED STATES	June 24	Fri.	NOON	—	June 29	June 29	—
AMERICA	June 30	Thurs.	4 P.M.	July 6	July 7	July 7	July 8
UNITED STATES	July 8	Fri.	NOON	—	July 13	July 13	—
UNITED STATES	July 21	Thurs.	NOON	—	July 26	July 26	—
AMERICA	July 22	Fri.	4 P.M.	July 28	July 29	July 29	July 30
UNITED STATES	Aug. 5	Fri.	NOON	—	Aug. 10	Aug. 10	—
AMERICA	Aug. 12	Fri.	4 P.M.	Aug. 18	Aug. 19	Aug. 19	Aug. 20
UNITED STATES	Aug. 18	Thurs.	NOON	—	Aug. 23	Aug. 23	—
UNITED STATES	Sept. 1	Thurs.	NOON	—	Sept. 6	Sept. 6	—
AMERICA	Sept. 2	Fri.	4 P.M.	Sept. 8	Sept. 9	Sept. 9	Sept. 10
UNITED STATES	Sept. 15	Thurs.	NOON	—	Sept. 20	Sept. 20	—
AMERICA	Sept. 23	Fri.	4 P.M.	Sept. 29	Sept. 30	Sept. 30	Oct. 1
UNITED STATES	Sept. 28	Wed.	NOON	—	Oct. 3	Oct. 3	—
UNITED STATES	Oct. 11	Tues.	NOON	—	Oct. 16	Oct. 16	—
AMERICA	Oct. 14	Fri.	4 P.M.	Oct. 20	Oct. 21	Oct. 21	Oct. 22
UNITED STATES	Oct. 25	Tues.	NOON	—	Oct. 30	Oct. 30	†Oct. 31
UNITED STATES	Nov. 9	Wed.	NOON	—	Nov. 14	Nov. 14	†Nov. 15
AMERICA	Nov. 18	Fri.	4 P.M.	Nov. 24	Nov. 25	Nov. 25	Nov. 26
UNITED STATES	Nov. 25	Fri.	NOON	—	Nov. 30	Nov. 30	†Dec. 1
AMERICA	Dec. 9	Fri.	NOON	Dec. 15	Dec. 16	Dec. 16	Dec. 17
UNITED STATES	Dec. 10	Sat.	NOON	—	Dec. 15	Dec. 15	—
				1961	1961	1961	1961
AMERICA	Dec. 30	Fri.	NOON	Jan. 5	Jan. 6	Jan. 6	Jan. 7

(Rows from Apr. 27 to Aug. 18 bracketed: Summer Season Rates Apply)

†All Passengers Debark on Arrival

WESTBOUND from Europe

VESSEL	Leave Bremerhaven	Leave Southampton P.M.	Leave Havre A.M. Embarkation Previous Evening	Leave Cobh P.M.	Due New York, New York Time: Date	Day	Hour
UNITED STATES	*Mar. 19	Mar. 20	Mar. 21	—	Mar. 25	Fri.	A.M.
AMERICA	†Mar. 28	Mar. 29	Mar. 30	Mar. 30	Apr. 5	Tues.	A.M.
UNITED STATES	*Apr. 5	Apr. 6	Apr. 7	—	Apr. 11	Mon.	A.M.
AMERICA	†Apr. 18	Apr. 19	Apr. 20	Apr. 20	Apr. 26	Tues.	A.M.
UNITED STATES	—	Apr. 20	Apr. 21	—	Apr. 25	Mon.	A.M.
UNITED STATES	*May 4	May 5	May 6	—	May 10	Tues.	A.M.
AMERICA	†May 9	May 10	May 11	May 11	May 17	Tues.	A.M.
UNITED STATES	—	May 18	May 19	—	May 23	Mon.	A.M.
AMERICA	†May 30	May 31	June 1	June 1	June 7	Tues.	A.M.
UNITED STATES	—	June 1	June 2	—	June 6	Mon.	A.M.
UNITED STATES	—	June 15	June 16	—	June 20	Mon.	A.M.
AMERICA	†June 20	June 21	June 22	June 22	June 28	Tues.	A.M.
UNITED STATES	—	June 30	July 1	—	July 5	Tues.	A.M.
AMERICA	†July 10	July 11	July 12	July 12	July 18	Mon.	A.M.
UNITED STATES	—	July 14	July 15	—	July 19	Tues.	A.M.
UNITED STATES	—	July 27	July 28	—	Aug. 1	Mon.	A.M.
AMERICA	†Aug. 1	Aug. 2	Aug. 3	Aug. 3	Aug. 9	Tues.	A.M.
UNITED STATES	—	Aug. 11	Aug. 12	—	Aug. 16	Tues.	A.M.
AMERICA	†Aug. 22	Aug. 23	Aug. 24	Aug. 24	Aug. 30	Tues.	A.M.
UNITED STATES	—	Aug. 24	Aug. 25	—	Aug. 29	Mon.	A.M.
UNITED STATES	—	Sept. 7	Sept. 8	—	Sept. 12	Mon.	A.M.
AMERICA	†Sept. 12	Sept. 13	Sept. 14	Sept. 14	Sept. 20	Tues.	A.M.
UNITED STATES	—	Sept. 21	Sept. 22	—	Sept. 26	Mon.	A.M.
UNITED STATES	—	Oct. 4	Oct. 5	—	Oct. 9	Sun.	A.M.
AMERICA	†Oct. 3	†Oct. 5	●Oct. 4	Oct. 5	Oct. 11	Tues.	P.M.
UNITED STATES	—	Oct. 17	Oct. 18	—	Oct. 22	Sat.	A.M.
AMERICA	†Oct. 24	Oct. 25	Oct. 26	Oct. 26	Nov. 1	Tues.	A.M.
UNITED STATES	*Nov. 1	Nov. 2	Nov. 3	—	Nov. 7	Mon.	A.M.
UNITED STATES	*Nov. 16	Nov. 17	Nov. 18	—	Nov. 22	Tues.	A.M.
AMERICA	†Nov. 28	Nov. 29	Nov. 30	Nov. 30	Dec. 6	Tues.	A.M.
UNITED STATES	*Dec. 2	Dec. 3	Dec. 4	—	Dec. 8	Thurs.	A.M.
AMERICA	†Dec. 19	Dec. 20	Dec. 21	Dec. 21	Dec. 27	Tues.	A.M.
UNITED STATES	—	Dec. 16	Dec. 17	—	Dec. 21	Wed.	A.M.
	1961	1961	1961	1961	1961		
AMERICA	†Jan. 9	Jan. 10	Jan. 11	Jan. 11	Jan. 17	Tues.	A.M.

(Rows from United States, June 30 to America, Oct. 24 bracketed: Summer Season Rates Apply)

*Embarkation Same Day
†Embarkation Previous Evening

●Call Havre Prior Southampton This Voyage Only

No. 2 March 1960 — AND REGULARLY THEREAFTER

A huge banner proclaims, 'Welcome SS *United States*' on 3 July 1952. Every building along the waterfront of New York was specially dressed ready for the noon departure of the SS *United States* on her maiden voyage. For a few days prior to her departure the great liner had an open house to curious visitors, excited prospective passengers and reporters who went aboard to explore the national pride of America. (Britton Collection)

⬐ First sight! Excited crowds throng at the Battery to catch a first glimpse of the SS *United States* outbound on her maiden voyage across the Atlantic to Europe on Wednesday 3 July 1952. (Britton Collection)

⬐ On a sound colour film taken at this exact point at the time on Wednesday 3 July 1952, a child is heard to call out, 'Wow! She's awesome.' A lady shouts, 'God bless the *United States*.' Spontaneous cheers and applause from the excited gathered crowd then break out. (Britton Collection)

60

⇗ A striking view of the outbound SS *United States* on her eastbound record-breaking maiden voyage. Smoke can be seen drifting from the aft funnel as the steam turbines engage to full power using the quadruple screws. (Britton Collection)

⇙ The excited crowds watch with awe and wonder as the SS *United States* slowly passes. It was expected to be a record run on the maiden voyage and luckily the weather conditions were almost perfect on Wednesday 3 July 1952. (Britton Collection)

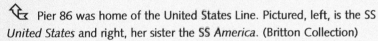 Pier 86 was home of the United States Line. Pictured, left, is the SS *United States* and right, her sister the SS *America*. (Britton Collection)

⤴ The SS *United States* at her New York home, Pier 86 at West 46th Street. (Britton Collection)

⤴ Crowds watch the departure of the SS *United States* from every vantage point along Pier 86 and on board. The Moran tug begins to heave and take the strain as the ropes are let go to indicate that the world's fastest ocean liner is now free. Pictured on the left is the cruise liner *Olympia*. Built in 1953 by Alexander Stephen & Sons, Glasgow, Scotland, she was designed to operate regular transatlantic voyages from Piraeus to New York, although later from 1961 she became a seasonal cruise ship. (Britton Collection)

62

↖ A bird's-eye view of the SS *United States* at Pier 86 and her British rival the Cunard RMS *Queen Elizabeth* at Pier 90. (Harvey Sharman Collection)

↴ The two 35ft-high funnels of the SS *United States* dominate the skyline above Pier 86. (Britton Collection)

A focused view of the forward section of the SS *United States* at Pier 86. (Britton Collection)

The Harman family, seated on their luggage, patiently await their turn at the United States Line passenger check in ready to board the SS *United States* for an eastbound voyage to Europe in 1962. (Art Harman Collection)

The United States Line Pier 86 passenger hall is packed with excited passengers, relatives and friends in this 1962 view. Quite often the thrill of the occasion was added to by a serenading band playing music as passengers boarded the SS *United States*. (Art Harman Collection)

↖ This is a street-level view of loading aboard the SS *United States* with the separate gangways for each class: first, cabin and tourist. Note the red-coloured flat-bottom timber bumpers that separated the huge liner from the pier pilings. (Bill Cotter Collection)

↙ One of the most famous signs along the waterfront of New York, 'United States Line SS *United States* Sailing Noon Today', read by thousands, but rarely photographed. (Britton Collection)

At 11.30 a.m., a full thirty minutes before sailing, the powerful, deafening Tyfon whistles of the SS *United States* would sound three times and the call would go out, 'all ashore that's going ashore'. Visitors would then scramble on to Pier 86 to wave their final farewells. (Britton Collection)

The Harman family gaze at the Empire State Building and the Manhattan skyline from the deck of the SS *United States* in 1962. (Art Harman Collection)

The razor-sharp, streamlined stem of the bow of SS *United States* was a triumph of marine engineering. (Dave Witmer/Britton Collection)

Underneath the stem was the huge forward anchor of the SS *United States*, seen here at New York's Pier 86 in October 1960. (Dave Witmer/Britton Collection)

↖ The Leslie Tyfon whistle attached to the forward funnel booms out three times to announce to New York that the SS *United States* is sailing. (Dave Witmer/Britton Collection)

↙ With the assisting Moran tugboat safely attached, there is time to focus on the proud white name letters 'United States' on the bow of the great liner. (Britton Collection)

⬇ The futuristic design of the radar mast is complemented by the fine display of flags. From the keel to the top of the structure was 122ft. (Dave Witmer/Britton Collection)

↘ The SS *United States* measured 990ft in length, nearly five city blocks, and could travel 10,000 miles without stopping for fuel, water or supplies. Viewed from sea level at Pier 86 in New York, it was possible to appreciate something of her enormous size. (Dave Witmer/ Britton Collection)

This fascinating picture of the SS *United States* moored at Pier 86 in New York shows several doors open on the side of the liner ready for connection to service vessels for fuel, sewage and general supplies. (Bill Di Benedetto Collection)

The Moran Towing Co. tugboat *Julia C. Moran* is buffered up ready to assist the SS *United States* at Pier 86 in New York on 29 July 1963. The Moran Towing & Transportation Co. was founded by Michael Moran in 1860 and was by far the largest towing company in the USA. The hard-working tugboats could easily be identified by the large white letter M painted on their black funnels and they were named after Moran family members.

Docking and undocking the giant liners like the SS *United States* in New York only accounted for a minor portion of the Moran Towing activities, but it was the most spectacular operation undertaken by the tugs. The small boats giving their all pushing and pulling the enormous ocean liners became a familiar everyday scene which was particularly cherished by proud New Yorkers with the arrival and departure of the SS *United States*. (Britton Collection)

Slowly, inch by inch, the SS *United States* reverses out into the Hudson River assisted by fussing Moran tugs. The crew of the SS *Tarsus* on the right of the picture line the decks and cannot resist watching the proceedings. (Britton Collection)

The funnels of the SS *United States* can bee seen behind her older sister and running mate the SS *America*. She was launched on 31 August 1939 and delivered to her owners on 2 June 1940. Her maiden voyage commenced on 10 August 1940 with a cruise to the West Indies. However, with the interruption of the Second World War, the SS *America* did not cross the Atlantic in the role in which she was intended until 22 July 1946. In November 1964 United States Line sold the *America* to Chandris Line. Very sadly, her end came on 18 January 1994 when she ran aground, breaking in two off Fuerteventura in the Canary Islands whilst being towed to Thailand for use as a proposed floating hotel. (Britton Collection)

⬑ Look, no tugs! This was the result of an industrial dispute on 5 February 1964, but docking and undocking without tug assistance required great skill, concentration and patience from the captain and all the crew. (Robert Palmer Collection)

⬐ On 5 February 1964, the SS *United States* docked unassisted without tugs. During the docking manoeuvre a hawser snapped and the total delay was recorded as five hours. (Robert Palmer/Britton Collection)

72

A misty departure in the autumn of 1960 at Pier 86 shows the SS *United States* ably assisted by Moran tugs pushing her out gently in to the Hudson River. (Robert Palmer Collection)

The view aboard the SS *United States* at departure time in 1962. (Art Harman Collection)

A view of the scene at the outer end of Pier 86, taken from the departing SS *United States* shows family and friends throwing streamers, waving and cheering. The gigantic vessel gently glides past, appearing larger and more glamorous than ever to the spectators. (Britton Collection)

Looking back to Pier 86 from the SS *United States* which is by now well out in the Hudson. The spectators appear to be reluctant to leave and are eager to catch a final glimpse of passengers aboard the 'Big U'. (Britton Collection)

A dramatic smoky departure from Pier 86 in New York. In August 1952 a written warning for smoke emission was served on the United States Line regarding the SS *United States*. A further warning was served against the United States Line on 27 April 1953, following observations made by Dr Leonard Greenburg, commissioner of the New York Department of Air Pollution, that the forward funnel had made thick black smoke for ten minutes as the liner passed through the Upper Bay. Despite measures to clean up and prevent smoke emissions, the SS *United States* continued to have a reputation for dramatic black smoke emissions on both sides of the Atlantic. (Britton Collection)

The SS *United States* is pictured in the Hudson River having departed from Pier 86 at New York. She is now in the process of the turn manoeuvre to position her towards the Upper Bay, the Narrows and the north Atlantic. (Bill Di Benedetto Collection)

Outbound on a cruise to St Thomas and dressed to perfection, the SS *United States* looks stunning on Voyage 339 on 4 March 1967. She is ably assisted by two Moran towing tugboats out into the Hudson. The industrious Moran tugs would haul on thick hawsers and cross her bows at speed when the SS *United States* majestically turned. (Richard Weiss Collection)

⬉ With a backdrop of Manhattan, the SS *United States* is pictured departing from Pier 86 at New York. (Pierrick Roullet, World Ship Society, Paris, France)

⬋ This picture oozes atmosphere, with a suitable backdrop of the Empire State Building and New York City, and shows passengers lining the decks to wave their final farewells to friends and family, as the SS *United States* begins to slowly turn in the Hudson on 21 May 1953. (Britton Collection)

Taken from a pleasure craft, this picture shows the SS *United States* on her final turning sequence in the Hudson before heading out of New York. The United States Line produced some wonderful plastic models of the great liner, which small boys the world over sailed in their baths to replicate this picture! The author always ensured his model *United States* was present for bath times. (Britton Collection)

A plume of smoke is emerging from both funnels to indicate that the SS *United States* is now almost independently underway as the Moran tug begins to drop away, having exerted pressure against the great ship's side. More aluminium was used in the construction of the SS *United States* than in any other single structure on land or sea. It was often quoted that the only wood on the liner was in the grand piano and the butcher's block! (Britton Collection)

The SS *United States* is in the final stages of her swing manoeuvre having departed from Pier 86. The crew of the SS *Tarsus* have now made their way to the stern of their ship to watch the departure. (Britton Collection)

In this superb view taken in December 1960, we can see the rival Cunard RMS *Queen Mary* has slipped out from Pier 92 ahead of the SS *United States* and is passing between the end of the piers outbound for Europe. (Britton Collection)

⬆ Exactly twenty-one minutes have passed since the previous picture was taken; photographed from the same position, the SS *United States* is now in pursuit of the Cunard RMS *Queen Mary*, following her down the Hudson in December 1960. (Britton Collection)

⬆ The SS *United States*, affectionately known as the 'Big U', weighed 51,987 tons with a draught of 28ft 6in, a length of 990ft (over three football pitches in length) and a height of seventeen storeys. Here we see her gracefully gliding down the Hudson towards the Upper Bay and the Atlantic Ocean, escorted by a Moran tug. (Britton Collection)

Majestic and magnificent, a midships view of the stupendous mighty funnels of the SS *United States* as she heads down the Hudson. (Mick Lindsay Collection)

A classic view, taken heading down the Hudson, from the stern of the SS *United States*. (Britton Collection)

↗ With a Manhattan backdrop, the SS *United States* cautiously makes her way through Upper New York Bay towards the Narrows in April 1959. (Britton Collection)

↘ An on-board view from the SS *United States* of the outbound approach to the Verrazano Narrows Bridge. Beyond is the challenge of the Atlantic Ocean and an unknown adventure aboard the fastest liner in the world. (Britton Collection)

With the Stars and Stripes flag gently fluttering from the stern of the ship, the SS *United States* increases speed to full ahead now she is out into the Atlantic in this picture taken in September 1961. The coast of the United States gently fades into the mist. (Britton Collection)

⭑ Soon after sailing, the routine was to have a lifeboat drill for all passengers and crew. The Harman family are all prepared with their lifejackets on. (Art Harman Collection)

⭑ With the SS *United States* now out at sea, it is time to have some fun. The Harman family are photographed in their cabin on the top bunk blowing up some United States Line balloons. (Art Harman Collection)

⭑ Next the Harman family go aft to the stern of the great liner to release balloons to drift above the wake of the ship into the Atlantic. (Art Harman Collection)

Once at sea, the SS *United States* had a great sense of speed, urgency and purpose. When the liner began to get into her stride at a speed of in excess of 33 knots, the wind would howl and whistle and so this position on the boat deck next to the funnels was an ideal place. Those huge red funnels made an impressive sight on the top decks in this picture taken in September 1961. (Britton Collection)

A lady passenger is seen lying on a towel taking advantage of the shelter from the wind. On the boat deck, in davits positioned all around the superstructure of the ship, were twenty-two aluminium lifeboats. (Britton Collection)

A picture of lifeboat No.2. The twenty-two aluminium lifeboats were non-sinkable and fully fireproof, with a combined accommodation of 3,000 persons. The maximum regular capacity of the SS *United States* was 1,800 passengers and 1,000 crew. (Britton Collection)

Look, but don't touch! Looking aft in September 1961, between the two kingpins, was a crew-only area packed with fascinating equipment. (Britton Collection)

It is shirt-sleeve weather in September 1961 and the aft deck is busy with sunbathing passengers, relaxing in the aluminium deckchairs and playing shuffleboard. (Britton Collection)

The classic aluminium deckchairs have been abandoned in favour of some deck games. (Britton Collection)

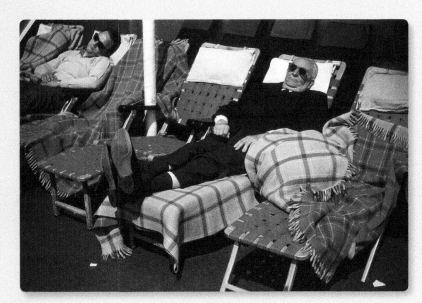

Two gentlemen enjoy a well-deserved rest in the sunshine relaxing in the classic SS *United States* aluminium deck chairs. (Britton Collection)

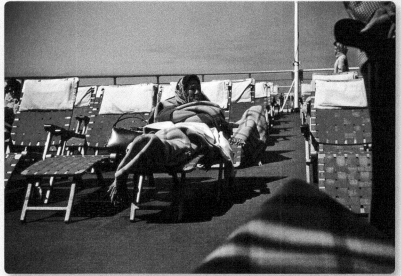

Passengers had to wrap up well on the exposed decks of the SS *United States* as, although it may appear sunny, there was effectively always a headwind due to the speed of the liner. (Britton Collection)

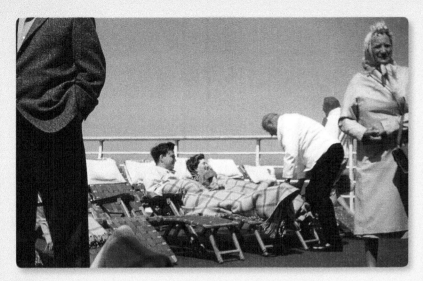

First-class passengers were pampered by dedicated deckchair stewards who looked after their every need, including tucking them up in a blanket. (Britton Collection)

The deck steward is busy serving refreshments to passengers on the open sun deck promenade. On the SS *United States* he would serve passengers from a choice of thirty-seven different champagnes and 134 wines. (Britton Collection)

The Harman family try their hand at shuffleboard. (Art Harman Collection)

86

Do we have a winner in the Harman family SS *United States* shuffleboard game of 1962? (Art Harman Collection)

Racing aft across the decks on the SS *United States*. (Art Harman Collection)

After the athletic fun on deck, there is a chance for the Harman family to relax in the SS *United States'* deck chairs. (Art Harman Collection)

A deserted aft deck whilst steaming for England in 1962, but the smoke is still pouring out of those huge red funnels. (Art Harman Collection)

A mid-Atlantic view from the stern of the ship shows a trail for miles of white wake and smoke. The logbooks record that during a cruise the SS *United States* was delayed by high winds, but being the fastest ocean liner afloat, as soon as the wind speed declined she compensated for this by accelerating to over 37 knots in order to reach the next port of call on schedule. (Art Harman Collection)

This cosy and delightful first- and cabin-class theatre seated 352 persons. The stage curtains were hand-woven with pompoms to create a carnival atmosphere. Vertical wall panels, a tiled roof and thick carpeting were designed to provide excellent acoustics. The projection and screen equipment for films allowed for wide-screen cinemascope in stereo. (United States Line)

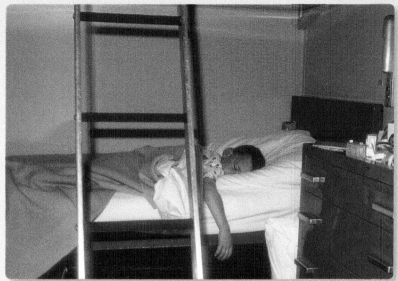

The Harman family have a party in the children's playroom on the Forward Upper Deck. This was one of three well-equipped playrooms on the SS *United States*. Designed by a child psychologist, each playroom had child-size furniture, lavatory facilities and a drinking fountain. Parents could relax and enjoy the liner's other facilities as trained play supervisors took good care of the youngsters. When parents came to collect their children, good behaviour reports were rewarded with soft ice creams smothered in strawberry sauce. (Art Harman Collection)

Good night Art! (Art Harman Collection)

The tourist-class smoking room located on the Forward Main Deck ran the full width of the ship and was equipped with a bar. A series of soft-coloured maps in fireproof aluminium frames added wall interest. The floor was made of a treated fire-proof marbled rubber, which was easy on the feet and eyes. (United States Line)

⬑ At the entrance to the first-class observation lounge and library was a colourful mural depicting the Atlantic Ocean. It was called *The Currents* and was painted on aluminium panels. The continents were painted in gold leaf, while the ocean was painted in various shades of blue and green. The directions of currents were highlighted using dimensional arrows. Whenever my family visited the SS *United States* when she docked in Southampton, my father, who was a geography teacher, gave an impromptu lesson about sea currents at this point. (Britton Collection)

⬐ This beautiful aerial view of the SS *United States* shows her cutting through the waves of the Atlantic with ease. Throughout her active career, this ocean greyhound never encountered any serious mechanical difficulty and was a great testimony to her revolutionary designer William Francis Gibbs. According to the ship's crew, when the liner was due to arrive he would drive his limousine to Shore Parkway in Brooklyn to watch her sail through the Narrows and under the Verrazano Bridge. Mr Gibbs' chauffeur would then whisk him smartly down to Pier 86 to observe the docking. The liner's designer would next go aboard the 'Big U' and make for the captain's cabin to discuss the completed voyage and thereafter call in to see Chief Engineer Bill Kaiser. William Francis Gibbs was always present at departures and frequently telephoned the ship to check on progress when at sea. (United States Line)

⇗ The SS *United States* is in the process of her swing manoeuvre at Le Havre. The French tugs were presented with a real challenge and are pictured toiling hard, pushing and pulling with all their combined might. (Marc Piche Collection)

⇖ Well-wishers, friends and families eagerly await the arrival of the SS *United States* on the dock quay at Le Havre. The gangways are rolled out and waiting with a banner proudly proclaiming 'United States Line'. Viewed from on board the SS *United States* in 1961 is the 575m-long Transatlantique Du Havre terminal building. (Britton Collection)

⇗ Passengers on board the SS *United States* watch and photograph the docking of the liner at Le Havre. The crane jibs are standing to attention but will soon be in action unloading once the liner is safely docked. (Britton Collection)

⇗ The tide is out at Ryde Pier on the Isle of Wight. At the end of the pier, steam-hauled trains are waiting to depart to Cowes and Ventnor. Meanwhile the SS *United States* passes slowly, having picked up the pilot at the Nab Tower off Bembridge. (Britton Collection)

⇗ The inbound SS *United States* passes the outbound Cunard RMS *Carmania* at the Spithead between Ryde and Portsmouth in June 1964. The Spithead fort, on the right of the picture, was built in the 1860s to protect maritime access to Portsmouth and bombardment from the sea. There are four of these forts: Spit Bank Fort, Horse Sand Fort, St Helens Fort and No Mans Land Fort. (R.J. Blenkinsop)

Viewed from the shores of the Isle of Wight at Cowes, the SS *United States* is seen gently making her way towards Egypt Point ready to turn sharply off Calshot. In April 1957 the United States Line was prosecuted for damaging the property of an English holidaymaker; namely, destruction of her picnic. She alleged that this had been caused by the wash coming up the beach from the SS *United States* due to excessive speed as the liner passed Netley Shore. The case was proved and compensation was awarded for the magnificent sum of £2 and 15 shillings at Southampton Magistrates Court. Justice of the Peace H. Watson further warned the United States Line about observation of speed restrictions and good conduct of the captain of the SS *United States*. (David Peters)

Summer holidaymakers at Cowes on the Isle of Wight pause to observe the passing of the SS *United States* up the Solent in September 1969. The driver of the Ford Corsair car is diving into his boot to retrieve his camera to record the occasion. (R.J. Blenkinsop)

⇐ This and the following three images show a unique sequence of the inbound SS *United States* passing the flagship of the Cunard Line, the 83,673-ton RMS *Queen Elizabeth*, outbound for Cherbourg and New York. These rare action shots were taken from a Blue Funnel pleasure boat off Hythe Pier in 1968. The fastest passenger ocean liner in the world is passing the largest passenger ocean liner in the world. (All images Barry Eagles Collection)

The SS *United States* is closely escorted by an armada of Red Funnel and Alexander Towing Co. tugs. She is now under the direction of the Trinity House pilot as she passes the Royal Pier at Southampton. (Britton Collection)

With the Red Funnel tug tender *Calshot* tucked in to the starboard side and a brace of Alexander Towing Co. tugs leading the way, the SS *United States* heads past Mayflower Park at Southampton, heading for 107 Berth in the New Docks. (Mick Lindsay Collection)

With a Red Funnel tug tucked into the starboard side and Alexander Towing Co. tugs leading the way, the SS *United States* heads for 107 Berth in the New Docks on 1 July 1961. A fine parade of liners is berthed in the New Docks, including at least two Union Castle Line ships and the P&O Line *Oriana*. (George Garwood/World Ship Society)

As the SS *United States* passes, two Union Castle liners are seen being loaded in the New Docks awaiting sailing to South Africa, one of which is the *Windsor Castle*, at 101 Berth. (Mick Lindsay Collection)

The pride of the United States Line, the SS *United States* makes her way past Mayflower Park, Southampton, in the care of a flotilla of Red Funnel and Alexandra Towing Co. tugs on 1 October 1962. The port of Southampton was known as the 'Gateway to the World' and benefited from a double tide, which was used to great advantage by ocean liners. (Austen Harrison/World Ship Society)

The arrival of the SS *United States* never failed to disappoint. The passengers of the pleasure craft have a ring-side seat on 1 October 1962. A brace of Red Funnel and Alexandra Towing Co. tugs lead the 'Big U' into Southampton followed by another Alexandra Towing tug at the stern. (Austen Harrison/World Ship Society)

A telescopic lens view of the arrival of the SS *United States* on 1 October 1962 watched by a packed pleasure boat which has a grandstand view. (Austen Harrison/World Ship Society)

Passengers on the starboard side deck of the SS *United States* catch a glimpse of the Cunard RMS *Queen Elizabeth* in the King George V Dry Dock at Southampton, whilst docking in 1955. (Britton Collection)

This is a view from the bows looking towards Redbridge and the Test Estuary as the 'Big U' is docked. Taking the strain of the 51,987-ton SS *United States* in 1960 are, from left to right: Alexandra Towing Co. tug *Gladstone*, Alexandra Towing Co. *Flying Kestrel* and Red Funnel *Hamtun*. (Britton Collection)

The British Union Flag and the Stars and Stripes of the USA greet the arrival of the SS *United States* at 107 Berth in Southampton in 1960. The United States Line gangways are ready and waiting on the dock side for attachment as soon as she is safely docked. (Britton Collection)

With the loading hatches open, the hard-working crew of the SS *United States* are pictured in action in the scene at Ocean Dock, Southampton. The 9in ropes were 120 fathoms in length and weighed about 18 cwt with a breaking strain of 31½ tons. The crew were always very friendly and ready to exchange a kind word in response to questions. (Britton Collection)

Waiting at the dockside was a fleet of cars ready to whisk celebrity passengers away from the
SS *United States*. Their drivers are no doubt seeking refreshments in the nearby Ocean
Restaurant, next to the red telephone box. (Britton Collection)

There were three complete sets of linen aboard the SS *United States*. Additionally, one set of linen was at the laundry at New York and one at the laundry in Southampton. Soon after arrival at Southampton, 'the dirties' were unloaded ashore. The average number of bags of soiled linen landed per voyage was 650 bags, both at New York and Southampton. In early 1969, the cousin of the author, Anthony Webb, was summoned urgently onto the SS *United States* immediately after docking at Southampton to repair a broken drum in the on-board laundry. He recalls working continuously until the job was completed minutes before sailing. Commodore Alexanderson came down personally to thank Anthony for rectifying the problem. (Gwyilym R. Davies/Britton Collection)

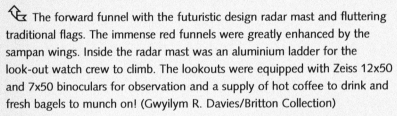

🖝 The forward funnel with the futuristic design radar mast and fluttering traditional flags. The immense red funnels were greatly enhanced by the sampan wings. Inside the radar mast was an aluminium ladder for the look-out watch crew to climb. The lookouts were equipped with Zeiss 12x50 and 7x50 binoculars for observation and a supply of hot coffee to drink and fresh bagels to munch on! (Gwyilym R. Davies/Britton Collection)

🖝 Who are the two traditionally helmeted British bobbies from the British Transport Police waiting for? They are standing dockside at Ocean Terminal, Southampton, waiting for the SS *United States* to dock. (John Goss)

🖝 While the Cunard Queens were away the SS *United States* docked in Ocean Dock, Southampton. It was from here that the legendry White Star Line ship RMS *Titanic* sailed to her sad fate. In this evocative picture on the opposite side of the dock the troop carrier SS *Empire Orwell* is looking the worse for wear, having just returned from Aden. (Britton Collection)

🖝 Viewed from the end of Ocean Dock on 17 July 1968, looking over an Alexander Towing Co. tug, the SS *United States* is almost perfectly framed. Note the painters are busy at work on a vessel to the right of the picture. (Austen Harrison/World Ship Society)

⤶ The SS *United States* is departing from the Ocean Dock bound for Le Havre on 20 July 1967. The group of fishermen on the edge of the dock seem almost oblivious to what is happening in front of their eyes, hoping to catch sea bass. On the right of the picture the stevedores have already positioned the portable gangways which are clearly lettered *Queen Mary*. When the picture was taken, she was due to arrive in just over an hour, so the SS *United States* was required to move off smartly. (Austen Harrison/World Ship Society)

⤷ Red Funnel and Alexandra Towing tugs push and pull the bow of the SS *United States* in the 180-degree swing positioning movement after departing from Ocean Dock. (Mick Lindsay Collection)

⤵ The fishermen have given up with their rods until the SS *United States* is clear of Ocean Dock. The Stars and Stripes flag is proudly displayed from the radar mast on 20 July 1967. Her Tyfon whistle could be heard as far away as Beaulieu Road Station in the New Forest and those gigantic red funnels could be seen from the Southampton Central railway station and the Civic Centre. (Austen Harrison/World Ship Society)

↖ A brace of Red Funnel tugs are pictured pushing and heaving the resplendent-looking SS *United States*. (John Goss)

↗ The Red Funnel diesel tug tender *Calshot* is seen pushing with all her might at the bow of the SS *United States*, under the command of Captain Steve Pascoe. The *Calshot* was the last tug tender to operate at the port of Southampton and was delivered in 1964 as a replacement for the steam-powered *Calshot* of 1930. By the mid-1960s, however, work for the tug tenders was rapidly diminishing and the new *Calshot* was converted to an oil dispersal vessel. To the right of the liner are the twin chimneys of Marchwood Power Station. (John Goss)

A brace of Red Funnel tugs are working hard at the bow end of the SS *United States* while a brace of Alexandra Towing tugs are heaving on their aft tow lines to swing around the stern. (John Goss)

This is the view at the Southampton Central railway station down platform with West Country Class steam locomotive 34045 Ottery St Mary with an express train for Bournemouth and Weymouth. The London Nine Elms shed engine crew have just handed over the controls of the Bulleid-designed steam locomotive to a Bournemouth crew and seem oblivious to the smoking funnels of the SS *United States*, which is about to sail. (Norman Roberts/Britton Collection)

A minute Alexandra Towing Co. tug nuzzles in alongside the SS *United States* prior to departure from 107 Berth. Note the gigantic floating crane pictured behind the liner. (Britton Collection)

⇖ This view was taken from the bridge of the Cunard RMS *Queen Mary* on 10 October 1967, showing the stern of the SS *United States* at 107 Berth and the Cunard RMS *Queen Elizabeth* preparing to sail from Ocean Dock. This was a very sad occasion as the RMS *Queen Mary* was being prepared for her last voyage to exile in Long Beach. (Austen Harrison/World Ship Society)

⇖ Peering across the stern of the SS *United States* with the Stars and Stripes flag proudly flying through the aluminium coloured king posts, derricks and life rafts, we can see that the three-funnelled Cunard RMS *Queen Mary* is preparing to sail from Ocean Dock bound for Cherbourg and New York. (Britton Collection)

↖ The engines are turning as smoke billows from the forward funnel across 107 Berth at Southampton. The unique funnels were proudly illuminated by spotlights during the hours of darkness acting as a beacon across Southampton. On occasions, owing to their immense size, the funnels could act like gargantuan sails if a south-westerly wind blew up Southampton Water when the ship was arriving and departing. The logbook records confirm that on one occasion this resulted in her breaking loose and causing damage. (Britton Collection)

The calm after the storm at Ocean Dock, Southampton, on 8 August 1968. The SS *United States* looks almost lonely and forlorn after recovering from a rough trip after crossing the Atlantic. The hull looks as if it has seen better days and a visit to the dry dock at Newport News for a repaint cannot be far off. (Roy Kittle/World Ship Society)

A bow-on view of the SS *United States* showing her in the process of being swung around by Red Funnel and Alexandra Towing Co. tugs. (Britton Collection)

This sea-level spectacular action shot, taken on 20 July 1967, shows an unidentified Alexandra Towing Co. tug on the left-hand side of the picture heaving a taught bow tow line with all her might. Meanwhile, the Red Funnel tug *Sir Bevois* is exerting her full power against the bow of the SS *United States* from her 1,500hp triple expansion engines. (Austen Harrison/World Ship Society)

106

⬀ The team work of tugs is on display as three Alexandra Towing Co. tugs are pictured in March 1958 easing the SS *United States* out of 107 Berth in the Southampton New Docks supported by a brace of Red Funnel tugs. (Gwyilym R. Davies/Britton Collection)

⬃ The screeching seagulls and the watching crew of the SS *United States* appear to be enjoying seeing the Red Funnel tug *Sir Bevois* working hard to turn the giant liner at Southampton on 20 July 1967. (Austen Harrison/World Ship Society)

⬃ The unrivalled serene beauty of the SS *United States*, visible in all her glory as she is gently turned by a brace of tugs after sailing from 107 Berth at Southampton in March 1958. (Gwyilym R. Davies/Britton Collection)

↖ This spectacular aerial view of the SS *United States* taken on 26 August 1954 shows her preparing to sail from 107 Berth at Southampton at 4.16 p.m. Two Red Funnel tugs buffer up forward and aft, while an Alexandra towing tug takes up position just off the bow. In the background is Millbrook railway station and the vast railway marshalling yards. (Pursey Short/Britton Collection)

↘ The next view, taken on 26 August 1954, shows that two further Alexandra Towing Co. tugs and one Red Funnel tug have joined the cavalcade to assist with the sailing of the SS *United States* from 107 Berth at Southampton. (Pursey Short/Britton Collection)

↖ Captain Jack Holt, the Trinity House pilot on board the SS *United States*, relays final commands to all hands and the captains on board the six assisting tugs: 'Make ready to sail.' (Pursey Short/Britton Collection)

↗ Docked ahead of the SS *United States* on 26 August 1954 was the Cunard luxury cruise liner RMS *Caronia*, popularly known as 'The Green Goddess'. (Pursey Short/Britton Collection)

With all tugs now in position, Trinity House Pilot Captain Jack Holt gives the order, 'Let go fore and aft,' on the 26 August 1954. (Pursey Short/Britton Collection)

Spectators wave and watch in anticipation on 26 August 1954 as the SS *United States* moves slowly away from 107 Berth. (Pursey Short/Britton Collection)

↖ Taken just a few seconds after the previous aerial picture with the sun now shining on the departure of the SS *United States*. (Pursey Short/Britton Collection)

↙ Ordered chaos! The six assisting Red Funnel and Alexandra Towing Co. tugs appear to be dancing around to new positions in order to escort the SS *United States*. (Pursey Short/Britton Collection)

A sea-level view of the departure of the SS *United States* in March 1958 with the Alexandra Towing Co. tug *Sloyne* leading the way. This tug was built in 1928 and weighed a mere 300 tons, but had 900hp. (Gwyilym R. Davies/Britton Collection)

With the hard part of the departure job done, the Red Funnel tugs break off to return to the New Docks for their next assignment. The SS *United States* is left to a brace of Alexandra Towing Co. tugs which lead the gleaming ship down Southampton Water towards Fawley in March 1958. (Gwyilym R. Davies/Britton Collection)

↖ Heading out of Southampton, the SS *United States* is escorted by two Red Funnel tugs, an Alexandra Towing Co. tug and a small pleasure boat packed with excited tourists in June 1965. (Pursey Short/Britton Collection)

↖ This spectacular aerial scene shows the SS *United States* being led away from the New Docks, Southampton, by a brace of Red Funnel tugs and an Alexandra Towing Co. tug on 26 August 1954. Behind her and a troop carrier ship is a steam locomotive, a former Southern Railway E1 Class tank engine, which is hauling full box vans to Southampton Terminus sidings. The landscape behind shows Millbrook and the reclaimed land, which has since changed dramatically after the construction of a modern container distribution centre. (Pursey Short/Britton Collection)

↖ The SS *United States* has passed Ocean Dock with the Ocean Terminal in clear view on 26 August 1954. This building was opened by the British Prime Minister, Clement Attlee, on 31 July 1950 at a cost of £750,000. It had a length of 1,297ft and the railway platform could handle two trains simultaneously. The SS *United States* used the Ocean Dock infrequently as it was usually reserved for the Cunard Queens. Behind is the Empress Dock. (Pursey Short/ Britton Collection)

↗ This impressive aerial view taken on 26 August 1954 of the SS *United States* sailing from Southampton reveals that she is being followed by four boat-loads of admirers, snapping action shots from their camera lenses. A beautiful reflection from the world's fastest ocean liner can be seen beside her. (Pursey Short/Britton Collection)

With a backdrop of Marchwood Power Station, the SS *United States* sails from the New Docks past the Royal Pier in Southampton. The Cunard RMS *Queen Elizabeth* can be seen docked at 108 Berth in October 1968. (Britton Collection)

Heading away down Southampton Water on 20 July 1967 towards Fawley led by a Red Funnel tug, the SS *United States* is admired by crowds of tourists from the vantage point of Town Quay, Southampton. (Austen Harrison/World Ship Society)

A magnificent collection of British vintage classic cars line up with their owners and passengers on Town Quay, Southampton, to watch the passing of the outbound SS *United States*. (Mick Lindsay Collection)

The SS *United States* is seen passing Fawley Oil Refinery, slowly heading down Southampton Water towards the Isle of Wight on 27 September 1967. (A.E. Bennett/Richard Clammer Collection)

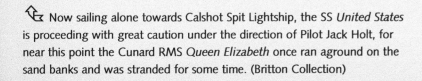

Now sailing alone towards Calshot Spit Lightship, the SS *United States* is proceeding with great caution under the direction of Pilot Jack Holt, for near this point the Cunard RMS *Queen Elizabeth* once ran aground on the sand banks and was stranded for some time. (Britton Collection)

Pictured off Calshot Spit, the SS *United States* looks magnificent. (Britton Collection)

'The Lady and the Liner'. A truly remarkable picture showing Isle of Wight steam locomotive 24 *Calbourne* preparing to depart from Cowes to Ryde, as the outbound SS *United States* traverses Cowes Roads on 24 October 1965. Note the chicken run on the right-hand side of the picture. The local signalman unofficially fenced off a section of the railway embankment, built a few wooden huts and provided all the local railway staff with a ready supply of fresh eggs. The O2 Class steam locomotive 24 *Calbourne* is now preserved in full working order at the Isle of Wight Steam Railway, operating lovingly restored Island vintage trains between Wootton, Haven Street, Ashey and Smallbrook Junction. (Roy Hobbs)

The outbound SS *United States* is seen passing a row of classic cars at Cowes, Isle of Wight. The drivers and passengers have left their vehicles and braved the rain to appreciate one of the finest views in the Solent. (David Peters)

The outbound SS *United States* is seen in the Solent heading towards Ryde and the Nab Tower. Here she will drop off Pilot Jack Holt and the liner will then be able to increase speed. (John Wiltshire)

The SS *United States* is pictured arriving at Columbus Quay, Bremerhaven, in 1955, assisted by a cluster of tugs. The 3,500ft-long Columbus Quay extends along the Weser River, dates from the 1920s and has been the best-known German ocean terminal. (Johannes Fleck/ Historisches Museum Bremerhaven)

118

A misty arrival, with the sun hiding in the cloud, for the SS *United States* at Columbus Quay in Bremerhaven. The 40ft water depth made the arrival and departure of the SS *United States* less dependant on the tides. (Johannes Fleck/Historisches Museum Bremerhaven)

Three uniformed German Customs officials and passengers patiently wait in the 2,500ft Marine Terminal at Columbus Quay at Bremerhaven as the SS *United States* docks. (Johannes Fleck/Historisches Museum Bremerhaven)

Passengers are awaiting friends and families travelling on the SS *United States* at Bremerhaven. The flags of Germany and the United States flutter in the breeze side by side. (Johannes Fleck/Historisches Museum Bremerhaven)

The viewing galleries in the Columbus Quay terminal building at Bremerhaven are packed to overflowing with excited well-wishers as the SS *United States* docks. On the quayside, the portable gangways and cranes are ready to spring into action. (Britton Collection)

German stevedores at Columbus Quay, Bremerhaven, safely attach the mooring ropes to secure the 51,987-ton SS *United States*. Each of the manila fibre ropes had a circumference of 9in, a weight of about 18 cwt and had a breaking strain of 31½ tons. (Johannes Fleck/Historisches Museum Bremerhaven)

The SS *United States* rests at Columbus Quay at Bremerhaven while the gantry cranes get to work. Each of these cranes had a 105ft reach and 8-ton capacity. On arrival, telescopic gangways marked 'United States Line' would project out to enable passengers to proceed to the Customs Hall and the waiting transcontinental express trains at the Marine Station. (Johannes Fleck/Historisches Museum Bremerhaven)

The SS *United States* is illuminated in nocturnal slumber at Columbus Quay at the Hanseatic city of Bremerhaven in 1955. (Johannes Fleck/Historisches Museum Bremerhaven)